COWLEY PUBLICATIONS is a ministry of the brothers of the Society of Saint John the Evangelist, a monastic order in the Episcopal Church. Our mission is to provide books and resources for those seeking spiritual and theological formation. Cowley Publications is committed to developing a new generation of writers and teachers who will encourage people to think and pray in new ways about spirituality, reconciliation, and the future.

ACQUAINTED WITH THE NIGHT

The Shadow of
Death in
Contemporary
Poetry

Jeffrey Johnson

Cowley Publications
Cambridge, Massachusetts

Library of Congress Cataloging-in-Publication Data:

Johnson, Jeffrey, 1959–
   Acquainted with the night: the shadow of death in contemporary poetry / Jeffrey Johnson.
      p. cm.
   Includes bibliographical references.
   ISBN 1-56101-251-3 (pbk.: alk. paper)
   1. American poetry–20th century–History and criticism. 2. Death in literature. 3. English poetry–20th century–History and criticism. 4. Thomas, R. S. (Ronald Stuart), 1913—Criticism and interpretation. 5. Berry, Wendell, 1934—Criticism and interpretation. 6. Hill, Geoffrey–Criticism and interpretation. 7. Cairns, Scott–Criticism and interpretation. 8. Jarman, Mark–Criticism and interpretation. I. Title.
   PS310.D42J64 2004
   811'.5093548–dc22
                        2003027529

Cover design: Jennifer Hopcroft
Cover art: Transcendence by Jae-Hee Hur, 2001. Oil on canvas. Used by permission.

This book was printed in the United States of America on acid-free paper.

Cowley Publications
907 Massachusetts Avenue
Cambridge, Massachusetts 02139
800-225-1534 • www.cowley.org

. . . I walk through the valley of the
shadow of death . . .
Psalm 23

. . . the hands of the sisters Death and Night
incessantly softly wash again, and ever again,
this soil'd world . . .
Walt Whitman (1819–1892)
Poems on the Civil War

I have been one acquainted with the night.
I have walked out in rain—and back in rain,
I have outwalked the furthest city light.

Robert Frost (1875–1963)
"Acquainted with the Night"

Table of Contents

Biographical Notes on the Poets

Wendell Berry has published nearly fifty books, including ten volumes of poetry, several novels, and many collections of essays on literature, agriculture, human community, and American culture. Before returning to Henry County in the Kentucky River Valley, where he was born in 1934 and where members of his family have farmed since the early nineteenth century, he taught and wrote at Stanford and at the City University of New York.

Scott Cairns is a professor of English, with research interests in Eastern Christianity, sacramental theology, and mystical religious traditions and poetics, at the University of Missouri-Columbia. Born in 1954 in Tacoma, Washington, his own Christian life journey has taken him from his family's Baptist church in Tacoma, to a Presbyterian congregation, to a Greek Orthodox church in Virginia. Cairns has published six books of poems.

Geoffrey Hill was born in 1932 in Worcestershire, England. He sang in the choir of his Anglican church from age seven until he left home for Keble College, Oxford, where he published his first poems. He taught at the University of Leeds and lectured at Cambridge as a Fellow of Emmanuel College. Hill has published ten books of poetry, two volumes of literary criticism, and a poetic dramatization of Ibsen's "Brand." Hill teaches English literature and religion in the University Professors' Program at Boston University.

Mark Jarman was born in 1952 in Mount Sterling, Kentucky. He grew up in England and in California and earned degrees at the University of California–Santa Cruz and the University of Iowa. He is the author of seven books of poetry and has edited collections of poems and books of criticism. A professor of English at Vanderbilt University, Jarman and his family live in Nashville, Tennessee.

R(onald) S(tewart) Thomas, the son of a sailor, was born in Cardiff, Wales in 1913. He studied classics at the University of Wales and theology at St. Michael's College. A priest of the Church of Wales, Thomas served rural parishes until his retirement in 1978. Writing in Welsh as well as in English, Thomas published twenty volumes of poems and received many honors and awards for his work. He died in 2000.

John Updike was born in 1932 in Shillington, Pennsylvania and is a graduate of Harvard College. Known primarily as a novelist of American suburban life, he has written many volumes of poetry, cultural commentary, and essays, on a wide array of subjects. Updike lives and writes in Beverly Farms, Massachusetts.

Introduction

By the tender mercy of our God,
  the dawn from on high will break upon us,
to give light to those who sit in darkness
  and in the shadow of death,
to guide our feet into the way of peace.

Luke 1:78–79

During those last weeks of the Bishop's life he
thought very little about death; it was the Past he
was leaving. The future would take care of itself.
But he had an intellectual curiosity about dying;
about the changes that took place in a man's beliefs
and scale of values. More and more life seemed to
him an experience of the Ego, in no sense the Ego
itself. This conviction, he believed, was something
apart from his religious life.
It was an enlightenment that came to him as a
man, a human creature.

Willa Cather (1873–1947)
Death Comes for the Archbishop

. . . the poem is not a statement but a performance
of forces, not an essay on life but a reenactment,
and just as people must search their lives over and
over again for the meaning of their deepest experi-
ences, so the performance of a true poem is endless
in being not a meaning but an act of existence.

John Ciardi (1916–1986)
How Does a Poem Mean?

Introduction

This book is a study of death as it appears in the work of a handful of contemporary poets. The commentary framing each poet's work includes observations by literary artists and critics, theologians, cultural critics, and scholars of religion. My objective has been to provide a Christian appreciation of each featured poet's work within a context of tradition and circumstances. I hope that readers of this book will return to the poets' published works, or turn to them for the first time. A list of suggested readings appears on page 157.

The main chapters, on the poems of Geoffrey Hill, Scott Cairns, Mark Jarman, R. S. Thomas, and Wendell Berry, contain comments about the general shape of each poet's work, but the primary focus throughout is directed to the appearance of death, and to the physical and metaphorical darkness often associated with the thought of death, in their poems. Readers might keep these two questions in mind:

- How do some of our best poets reflect death in their opaque art?
- What do their death poems tell us about our lives, about our faith—and the objects of our faith—and about the shape of our doubt?

The chapters are ordered in the way of a walk. Looking at one poet brings us within sight of another. Geoffrey Hill's scrupulous weighing of words and their implications leads to Scott Cairns's thought-serious poems. The dark humor in Cairns suggests a way into Mark Jarman's playful works. Jarman's contemplation of the hiddenness of God runs into R. S. Thomas's poetry of God's absence. Thomas's place-bound inspiration found in Welsh village life provides a bridge to Wendell Berry's love of the Kentucky land and the cycles of seasons on his farm.

Each of the chosen poets has been recognized by critics for his literary artistry. Each one also draws, a little or a lot, from the deep, wide well of faith and Christian tradition. None of them is presented as a model of faith. Readers should not assume that these poems stand as examples of doctrinal explication or spiritual inspiration. The poetry refers to death in ways that invite discussion and thought. Within these works lies a conviction of the inevitable failure of the flesh and a hope of love's consolation. Each poet fashions his art using themes, shards, and threads of the material of which faith is made. Readers equipped—however lightly—with the words of scripture and the mandates of faith may find in these poems terms of reference, rhythms, images, themes, and concerns that strike sympathetic chords.

Why *These* Poets?

Readers familiar with contemporary poetry are likely to ask how *these* five poets were chosen. They might wonder why Vassar Miller, Kathleen Norris, Louise Erdrich, Andrew Hudgins or Les Murray—to name another handful of accomplished contemporary poets who might have been profitably studied—were not included. Other readers might ask, if this is a book on death in contemporary poetry, where is an extended study of Seamus Heaney or of Louise Glück—or of any number of other contemporary poets whose works seem to be born in a less religious atmosphere—and *their* death lyrics? Or, why not an extended discussion of Donald Hall's poignant poems on the death of his wife, Jane Kenyon?

The answer is that in my personal, unsystematic reading, the poems of these five have held my attention long enough to inspire written responses of appreciation. In his essay "Poets, Critics and Readers," Randall Jarrell wrote, quoting Rainer Maria Rilke:

The work of art says to us always: You must change your life. It demands of us that we see things as ends, not as means—that we know them and love them for their own sake. The change is beyond us, perhaps, during the active, greedy, and powerful hours of our lives; but during the contemplative and sympathetic hours of our reading, our listening, our looking, it is surely within our power. . . .[1]

Jarrell goes on, encouraging us to "read at whim!" This book follows the whims of my own reading and is offered primarily to similarly interested readers.

While I am not able to judge the standing of the five chosen poets in a contemporary literary canon, I am willing to claim that Geoffrey Hill's linguistic morality and history-anguish; Scott Cairns's theological creations; Mark Jarman's lyric memories; R. S. Thomas's dark meditations; and Wendell Berry's local, planted perspective; taken together, provide a sufficiently full palate of colors to paint an accurate picture of mortality and death as viewed by literary artists today.

Poetry and Tradition

The Apostle Paul wrote that God's word is not chained.[2] Christians hear this theological declaration as good news, because we sense that our lives *are* chained in a number of ways: by personal and cultural history, by gender, geography, race, economic circumstances, and, of course, by the limitations of our flesh, including death. Poets also face constraints, working within received literary forms as the boundaries and measures of their art, even as they test and expand the limits of these forms. Poetry and other art are cultural products, and therefore are constrained by, or in dialogue with, the ways of a society. But a generation's best poets' words are not chained by political ideologies or by religious doctrine. While the best poems are written under responsibility to history—the history of language and the history of events—they are, as art, fundamentally free creations. Their peculiar power derives in large part from this artistic freedom.

Geoffrey Hill wrote of two of his predecessors—W. H. Auden and T. S. Eliot—that through the years they "worked increasingly within the disciplines of conscience [which are the] Christian principles of penitence and humility."[3] Probably a similar though not identical statement could be made about each of the poets included here. One may safely assume that at some time in each of their lives, probably early in their lives, these five became acquainted with Christian teaching, and probably with some form of piety and devotion, such as church or chapel attendance, and prayers at home. Therefore, as the Christian faith lives in their subconscious minds, it appears in their poetry, unbidden except by the requirements of artistic creation, and sometimes in surprising juxtaposition. For Christian readers, their poems may open up to a reading informed by faith.[4]

It should be admitted, however, that it is possible for a poet to have rejected conventional religious practice and still have a mind full of faith fragments. The poet's creations might be read profitably from a religious perspective, even if the poetry is not inspirational and does not seem to recommend a joyful apprehension of faith's assertions.

Faith cannot always interpret art. Art can hardly ever accept faith as a whole. Faith and art have a "push-me-pull-you" symbiotic relationship. The poet, as poet, is a priest of a distant altar, one that may not always serve the generally accepted divine order of life and devotion. While faith draws its adherents into an assembly or a community, art is often solitary. Like a restless child, art searches under rocks and in the crevasses of a tree's bark for clues to unknown questions. Faith invites those who gather to kneel for communion, to listen for the instruction they need for their lives. Art darts into the attic, or out into the churchyard, or into the alley, to poke around in a dark corner. As the push and pull of an exercise strengthens human muscles, the push and pull of faith and art may strengthen the human spirit of a given age.

T. S. Eliot thought that religion, over time, becomes petrified. The pressure of doctrine upon ritual and habit, over the years, compresses and deadens religious activity. He believed that religion could be refreshed by infusions of feeling, by new devotion, or by critical reason.[5] Any of these three renewing implements might be found in a good poet's toolbox.[6]

What Does a Poet Do?

A poet creates art in the medium of words. Yvor Winters wrote,

Poetry, as nearly as I can understand it, is a statement in words about human experience, whether the experience be real or hypothetical, major or minor; but it is a statement of a particular kind.[7]

The poets whose work appears here know well the lineage of the art they practice. We can tell, by their literary commentary as well as by their poems, that each has immersed himself in the history of language and of poetic form. Each has mastered the craft of combining content with form in the alchemy of producing a poem. With technical skill and with cultural, linguistic, and moral imagination, they accomplish their historical dredging and syntactical sculpting.

Often, poetry of the kind contemplated here is dismissed as inaccessible and is neither understood nor appreciated by large audiences. Poets kindle distant fires. They might keep the marketplace or the altar of the community church in mind, but normally they work on the edges of society. There they may recover what a culture has discarded—even what the culture is sure it never knew—yet needs to find again. It is up to us, the readers, to pick up what they have created, to listen to it, and examine it.

Although aspiring poets often gather for workshops or enroll in classes, a poet has a solitary vocation. Aware of what others have already said, each poet, writing out of a culture and a tradition, takes his or her own knowledge, understanding, emotional experiences, motivations, vices and virtues, and out of this mix creates a poem. Poems are not only discourses *about* human experience, they are also verbal memorials of what human experience *feels* like. The created works may also reflect the life or feelings of a friend or family member, the history of a race, of a nation, of women, of immigrants, or of any other group.

The Languages of Poetry and Faith

Poetry and faith meet as if they were cousins from distant lands who speak different languages. We may notice a family resemblance, but their clothing and customs, and especially their language, enable us to tell them apart. If the language of faith contains the believer's intention and assumptions about the nature of God,[8] then the language of poetry carries the poet's experience and understanding of the nature of language.

The literary poetry referred to here employs neither the *first order* faith language of witness and testimony, nor the *second order* language of theology. These two types of language constitute the language of faith. The church's liturgies, creeds, hymns, sermons, devotions, meditations, and confessions are examples and combinations of these two orders of religious language. The poetry explored here was written neither to be Christian testimony nor Christian apology. However, this kind of poetry may, by coincidence, share growing ground with religious faith. Both have roots in a mixture of organic memory held together with the stiffness of language and literary forms.

In critical reflection on the location of the boundaries between religion and poetry—between faith and art—the matter becomes more difficult. Thoughtful writers and careful scholars have tried to organize this field. Some have tried to differentiate between literary poetry and piety-laden religious poetry. They would separate literary poems of various kinds and traditions from the varieties of Christian, Jewish, or Islamic verse. In general, literary-critical standards will not permit the weight of doctrine, tradition, ethics, or piety to overbalance the linguistic and experiential freedom of a poem. In other words, if a poem is designed to reflect upon a religious experience, to package a doctrine as an aid to memory, or to call for justice from a religious perspective, it falls within the scope of religious poetry. Otherwise, it may be considered to be a literary work.

In his book *The Study of Literature and Religion*, David Jasper presents a reasoned view of the relationship between Christian belief and poetry. The points of his argument may be summarized as follows:

1. Poetry and religion, like oil and water, do not mix. Poets cannot reach the levels of divine truth given in scripture and doctrine; therefore Christian poetry must be a substratum of poetry. Conversely, Christian piety prevents the human imagination from the honest reaching that produces strong and lasting poetry. He cites Samuel Johnson, who called religious poetry "impertinence," as the proponent of the former reason, and Lord David Cecil, editor of the *Oxford Book of Christian Verse* (1940), who wrote that Christian poetry was "by its nature insincere," as the champion of the latter opinion.

2. Poetry that contemplates Christian doctrine, draws on biblical associations, theological patterns of thought, or contemplates virtues and feelings in terms of Christian belief may be written by persons who *are not* confessing Christians. Jasper offers poems by W. B. Yeats as examples of the work of a poet who drew on Christian material, among other sources, in his poetry but who was not an orthodox believer.

3. Poetry that contemplates Christian doctrine, draws on biblical associations, on theological patterns of thought, or contemplates Christian virtues may be written by persons who are confessing Christians. Here Jasper distinguishes poets such as Yeats and Rudyard Kipling on the one hand, from believing Christians such as George Herbert, Edwin Muir, and W. H. Auden on the other hand. Aware of a certain fallacy of intention—judging a poem by what we know or think we know about a poet—Jasper argues that poets such as Herbert, Muir, and Auden focused the substance of the Christian faith in contemporary and personal ways that those poets of uncommitted faith could not.

4. Poetry and religion intersect in the congregational hymn. Jasper writes that hymns are concerned with "Christianity in its public form, as doctrine. At their best, hymns are vehicles for a fine, sharp intellectualism, using compressed and clear language to express the concrete and particular matter of Christian belief."[9] While hymns have great influence on life and memory—and are almost certainly heard as distant echoes in some of the poetry presented here—as a genre the congregational hymn lies beyond the scope of the present study.

With a few exceptions, the poetry considered in the following chapters falls in and between Jasper's second and third categories. A case could be made that these two categories should be collapsed into one, with the first category, of religious verse, and the fourth, of the congregational hymn, remaining separate and distinct.

There are honored places for the inspiration and comfort given by the kind of "religious verse" that Samuel Johnson opposed. Verses of the kind that he had in mind have been carefully folded into daybooks and wallets and used for comfort and inspiration. In his introduction to *The New Oxford Book of Christian Verse*, Donald Davie refers to this kind of poetry as "devotional verse," and, while praising it for an individual's private religious use, omits it from his anthology. He writes that in making his choices for the anthology, he included only poems that measured up "strictly in artistry" to the best of the secular verse written during the same period.[10]

In a review of this Oxford anthology, John Updike commented on Davie's choices as well as on the poems themselves. Updike gives a valuable non-technical perspective on the joining of religion to poetry. The next chapter focuses not only on Updike's ideas about poetry and religion but also on Updike's own writing. He is, after all, one of the most celebrated contemporary American men of letters, bearing, sometimes uneasily, the mantle of a Christian writer. A look at how Updike has been perceived as a Christian writer, as well as how he construes the influence of religion on his own writing, will illustrate further the way religion and art intersect. This discussion will prepare the way for a review of death in contemporary poetry.

---

1. In R. S. Gwynn, ed., *The Advocates of Poetry* (Fayetteville: University of Arkansas Press, 1996), 220.

2. Timothy 2:9.

3. Geoffrey Hill, *The Lords of Limit, Essays on Literature and Ideas* (New York: Oxford University Press, 1984), 10.

4. For further discussion of reading from a perspective of faith see Robert Detweiler, *Breaking the Fall* (San Francisco: Harper & Row, 1989).

5. T. S. Eliot, *Selected Essays* (New York: Harcourt, Brace, 1951), 475.

6. Readers might look for the way conveyed feeling and new devotion operate in Thomas's, Hill's and Jarman's poems, which may not look like devotion at all; and for the way critical reason shapes Cairns's and Berry's poems.

7. Yvor Winters, *The Function of Criticism* (Norfolk: New Directions, 1943), 81.

8. See Louis Dupré, *Symbols of the Sacred* (Grand Rapids: Wm B. Eerdmans, 2000), 65.

9. David Jasper, *The Study of Literature and Religion* (Minneapolis: Fortress Press, 1989), 10ff.

10. Donald Davie, ed., *The New Oxford Book of Christian Verse* (Oxford: Oxford University Press, 1981), xviii.

Chapter 1

So do not worry about tomorrow, for
tomorrow will bring worries of its own.
Today's trouble is enough for today.
Matthew 6:34

I have the persistent sensation, in my life
and art, that I am just beginning.
John Updike (b. 1932)
Self-Consciousness: Memoirs

When Christ calls a man, He bids him come
and die . . . but we do not want to die. . . .
Dietrich Bonhoeffer (1906–1945)
The Cost of Discipleship

Setting the Stage: Poetry and Faith

In a review of *The New Oxford Book of Christian Verse,* John Updike notes with wry surprise that in 1981 the "Oxford University Press still considers 'Christian verse' a viable category."[1] After examining the volume's contents, which range from the tenth through the mid-twentieth century, Updike concludes that

> in the chronological course of this anthology, [one can feel] the language lose sharpness and variety as the focus of the poets moves from the Biblical drama, naïvely accepted as fact and self-explanatory, to the inward drama of faith and introspection.[2]

This shift in focus resulted from the "Age of Reason," or the Enlightenment, which swept through western Europe in the seventeenth and eighteenth centuries. In its aftermath, subjective human experience began to serve as the source of moral authority and the basis of truth. The story of God as revealed in scripture no longer exerted a preeminent hold.

The Enlightenment

Within the Enlightenment the natural and physical sciences advanced dramatically. Scientific methods of acquiring knowledge encouraged questioning and exploration, rather than depending on divine authority. A scientific world view coalesced around the discoveries of Galileo, Copernicus, Johannes Kepler, and Isaac Newton. Philosophers joined scientists in developing ways of thinking about the world that sloughed off religious assumptions and authority. This modern view of human life was humanistic and naturalistic. By the end of the nineteenth century, inheritors of the Enlightenment such as Karl Marx and Sigmund Freud so thoroughly assumed the new world view that questions of God's existence—vital to earlier thinkers—fell completely outside their concern.

Literary writers also joined this paradigm shift. The nineteenth century saw the rise of the novel, a new genre of literature which narrated stories about ordinary human lives.

A Rift in Religious Thought

The world view signaled by the Enlightenment remains in large part our working stage; yet religious thinkers are aware that the seismic shifts caused by the Enlightenment produced a rift of the spirit, leaving a chasm in the landscape of religious thought. On one side of the chasm, the Bible still stands as the word of authority for all who will listen. On the other side, religion coexists with modern technology and the information age, both of which seem to have little in common with the concerns of the biblical world. The chasm between the two world views is an intellectual divide that often dismays those who would cross it.

Fundamentalist and literalist readers of the Bible prefer to remain on the pre-Enlightenment side, which they do by placing a fence around the scripture. They declare the words of scripture to be sacred and inviolable, removed from the organic processes of life and death built into living languages. Such religious people are often accused of refusing to move forward.

Contemporary religious poets are quick to acknowledge that they stand on this side of the Enlightenment divide. As artists working in words, they could not operate in a fundamentalist mode. The language itself resists such an artificial preservation. Furthermore, present poets who trade in religious material resist being lifted into spiritual contemplation, or anything resembling it, by insisting on naturalism: their feet are planted firmly on the ground of this world, in the sensory and emotional experience offered by the ordinary world. They are not spiritualists or throwback pietists, operating in a ghetto of old-fashioned thought.[3]

Much contemporary poetry that might be called Christian is written from the edge of the great chasm caused by the earthquake of the Enlightenment. The poets' words are broadcast over the rift, while imagined signals return that might be impulses of memory lodged in the spiritual DNA of the poets themselves. The human spirit remains dimly tuned to the old frequencies, to the ages of unquestioning faith and the comforting history of ancient cultures. The signals also speak of future oblivion, when individual cycles of sensate life will cease. Our individual and cultural cycles will inevitably fade into darkness. These two darknesses together provide much of the oblique inspiration of "Christian" poetry.

John Updike on Christian Poetry

Self-consciously standing near the brooding darkness of the spiritual chasm of the Enlightenment, Updike offers his own useful definition of Christian verse:

> The very purpose of Christian verse is to celebrate what is not manifest; it therefore denies itself those worldly colors that delight us in most poetry and relies for sensational content upon intimations that are delicate and elusive.[4]

Updike's phrase, "to celebrate what is not manifest," echoes Hebrews 11:1: "Faith is the assurance of things hoped for, the conviction of things not seen." Readers familiar with Updike's writing, especially with his fiction but also with his under-appreciated poems, might conclude that most of Updike's own work would not fit his definition of Christian verse. He writes as a realist, depending on "worldly colors." To borrow a phrase from the social scientists, Updike practices a kind of literary *thick description*. He praises the world by describing it in recreated literary packages. He is also not the kind of writer who seems to brood over things. If one can take the word broadly and expansively, he is a *joyful* writer. His writing resembles an outpouring of unreserved secular praise. Still, he acknowledges that in a world unordered by external authority, there is a pervasive emptiness, a blankness that the human mind, somehow dimly recalling such authority, cannot help but ponder with dread or with wonder.[5]

Updike observes in the final paragraph of his review that the language of contemporary Christian poetry is "led toward an edge where words dim." As poets cast backward through history in search of truth or inspiration, and look forward in time to the end of life, words lose their capacity to carry meaning. Language tends to trail into night. Our literary artists, including Updike, typically choose the strategy of resisting the temptation to speculate about these distant borderlands. They turn, in the Enlightenment way, to the things of this world.

One emblem of this naturalist creed may be found in Richard Wilbur's poem "Love Calls Us to the Things of This World."[6] Part of the poem reads:

> Yet, as the sun acknowledges
> With a warm look the world's hunks and colors,
> The soul descends once more in bitter love
> To accept the waking body, saying now
> In a changed voice as the man yawns and rises. . . .

For Wilbur, the sun still shines, but the voice of humanity has undergone a noticeable change; as the poets considered in this book would also acknowledge, the purview of contemporary Christian poetry is not revelation and not received doctrine. Today's poets do not speculate about heaven or about God's nature or will. They meditate on the sins and graces of ordinary life. They make their art out of the earth under their own feet. If contemporary Christian poets are theologians, they are theologians of the Incarnation.

Updike as a Christian Writer

A recent collection of essays edited by James Yerkes analyzes the religious aspects of Updike's work.[7] The collection opens with Updike's poem "Earthworm," which Updike considers to be his "best-felt statement on religion." The poem begins:

> We pattern our Heaven
> on bright butterflies,
> but it must be that even
> in earth Heaven lies.
>
> The worm we uproot
> in turning a spade

returns, careful brute,
to the peace he has made.

God blesses him; he
gives praise with his toil,
lends comfort to me,
and aerates the soil.

There is probably some degree of irony in Updike's request that "Earthworm" be given such prominence in Yerkes' volume. He must have known that it would be followed by a formidable stack of academic essays on his work, all of them heavy with the kind of self-serious analysis in which his own voluminous, wise, but informal, commentary rarely indulges.

The poem itself could be said to unfold in Updike's suburban New England backyard. There it imagines for us a lowly creature giving praise in the way that any creature gives praise: by doing what it was created and equipped to do. Through the worm's daily work, the soil opens up to receive the air it needs. Through this aeration, strangers—such as a gardener, passersby, or other creatures—are given assistance in their own work. The writer, in his daily work, opens up the world for readers and, through his art, aerates the reader's world in unexpected ways. "Earthworm" concludes:

Immersed in the facts,
one must worship there;
claustrophobia attacks
us even in air.

An organism such as an earthworm, in pursuing its paths through the soil, opens up the elemental earth to another element: the air. The aerated soil then serves the needs of other creatures and plants. In a similar way, human beings, "immersed in the facts" of life on earth, may aerate the soil of their ordinary lives through worship and creative exploration of their environment (as in poetry), thereby opening up spiritual "airways" of knowledge and wisdom.

Comprehending Death

As far as we know, human beings alone comprehend that life leads to death. Scientists are able to enumerate the biological and chemical facts as life turns to death. Beyond that, the contemplation of death moves away from the stories of earth into realms of imagination, seeming to be a matter for religion or for fairy tales. Those who have no facility for religious language are likely to have nothing to say on the matter. They might even believe, incorrectly, that the Christian faith, because it professes immortality, denies death.

The Christian faith does not deny death when it affirms life. It does not even *defy* death. One might more accurately say that the Christian faith knows death well. In its liturgies the church returns again and again to the grave, and so has mastered Death's name. Death, personified, as in the words of a hymn attributed to St. Francis, plays a role written into the story of life from the beginning. Death, doing its own proper work, gives praise:

And you, most kind and gentle death,
Waiting to hush our final breath,
Oh, praise him! Alleluia![8]

Yet, as creatures of the earth we cannot sustain the degree of faith shown by a saint such as Francis. We, like Updike, find ourselves momentarily inspired and flush with faith, then full of doubt, at the same time saint and sinner.

Updike on Death

At the very end of his finely understated essay entitled "On Being a Self Forever," Updike meditates on death:

Though the phrase "death wish" has passed from favor, there is that in us which seeks rest from the irritation and agitation of life. To be done with the dentist, with twinges and remorses and second thoughts. . . . The self is not only self-protective and self-extending. It can condone its own end—witness suicides, soldiers, saints. Love and drugs and a good political cause can loom as greater goods than one's own life. Like a heap of loose iron filings, we want to be magnetically lined up. Only a transcendent magnet can do this. "Decimate us!"[9]

Updike displays human belief-against-unbelief when he shows his own division of mind on death:

> In this interim of gaining and losing, it clears the air to disbelieve in death and to believe that the world was created to be praised. But I inherited a skeptical temperament. My father believed in science and my mother in nature. She looked and still looks to the plants and the animals for orientation. . . . [10]

On the one hand he claims the naturalistic, earthly realism of his parents, who represent neatly the twin poles of the Enlightenment. On the other hand, his own hard-won view, from his own experience, sounds something like faith.

By calling the span of human life "this interim," Updike participates in a perception of time known to readers of the Bible. In its pages we read of eras and cycles, beginnings and apocalypses, pilgrimages and establishments of shrines and cities, homeless wanderings and joyful homecomings. One round of life leads to another. Liturgical seasons shape these different kinds of time into an ordered whole. Those who have heard scripture's stories and have participated to some degree in a liturgical procession of seasons, are likely to have this pattern running through their thoughts about their own life.

Still, the world can be read in other ways. One can come to different conclusions about the meaning of life, or one can defer indefinitely any thought about ultimate meaning. Updike shows the double-mindedness known to most of us as we struggle to believe in what we cannot see and envision life in an unpredictable future.

By referring to his parents, Updike brings to mind the continuity of the generations. The self-protective, self-extending part of himself will live in his children, even as his parents have extended their own selves through him. Human life continues on the earth, as does non-human life, in evolving patterns of ecosystems and societies, driven by the force of biological regeneration. Yet human beings have an inkling, at least, of other forces at work in life.

Human society does not meet every human need. Each of us retains an individual consciousness, however small, that yearns for more than our often disappointing human institutions and associations can provide. When pressed to describe it, we tell of a gnawing spiritual hunger that cannot be entirely satisfied through work, or play, or relationships. Augustine knew this human restlessness as a dis-ease of the spirit. He wrote that the human heart was restless until it rested in God. It must have been this same state of mind that led Paul to write to the new Christians in Corinth that we know we are uneasy in the darkness of our world because we have "glimpsed" the light:

> For we know only in part, and we prophesy only in part . . .
> when I became an adult, I put an end to childish ways.
> For now we see in a mirror, dimly, but then we will see face
> to face.[11]

To live within this restless double-mindedess is to accept the biological facts of life and death, yet at the same time to envision "a new heaven and a new earth."[12] The Christian, through faith, takes the world for what it is, holds up sacred history as a guide, and treasures hope as a family inheritance.

Even the mind of a thoroughly empirical thinker—one who will not admit of anything beyond what can be proved—may sense a dull edge of the unknown. In the course of our lives we pass through shadows of ambiguity and unknowing. Following Updike, we might posit God's presence from within a skeptical fog, even as we live in the dark. Updike writes:

> Evidence of God's being lies with that of our own; it is on
> our side of the total disparity that God lives. In the light,
> we disown Him, embarrassedly; in the dark, He is our only
> guarantor, our only shield against death. . . . God is the
> dark sphere enclosing the pinpoint of our selves, an
> adamant bubble enclosing us, protecting us, enabling us
> to let go, to ride the waves of what is.[13]

Updike's readers know that he relishes the ordinary ways of sinful humanity. Riding "the waves of what is" could describe

both Updike's approach to writing, as well as the Enlighten-
ment creed that remains our culture's mantra. This phrase, and
the imaginative conception of God as an "adamant bubble,"
suggest a brief theological comment.

Imagination and the Incarnation

A grounded, earth-oriented approach to life, typical of con-
temporary poets, is consistent with the world view found in the
Gospels. The story that feeds the imagination of faith is *incar-
nate*; it comes to us in the body and blood of the earth. In John's
Gospel, the Word became flesh and dwelt *among us*. In the first
three Gospels, the kingdom of heaven is *at hand*. The nativity
of Jesus, his teaching and preaching, including his healings, his
passion and death, and the final affirmation of the world in the
resurrection comprise a full *earth-oriented* tale.

As the Gospels tell the story of Jesus they fill the senses.
Artists, poets, and all the faithful may draw on images of the
Bethlehem manger, flowers and wheat of the field, water from
desert wells, paths through the wilderness, wine at a wedding,
fish and bread on a hill. The Gospels never deny ordinary
bloody birth and death, especially that death on a skull-strewn
hill outside the walls of Jerusalem. Death is real in their authors'
eyes. The Gospels feel death as we feel it, as pain and absence.

Imagination and a Theology of the Cross

Martin Luther's theology of the cross may apply to this dis-
cussion of poetic imagination. Luther saw the cross as the
symbol of suffering and death, and therefore as the central fact
revealing God to humanity. For Luther, the cross meant that
God meets us in death.[14] God is known to the eyes of faith not
only under the suffering and death of Christ, when faith identi-
fies with Christ, but also under and through other forms of
appearance and thought, which are the veils and masks of God.
Haunted, tempted, and Christ-filled, Luther believed that God
could hide even under the form of the devil. The most full and
scandalous hiding of God was in the despised man Christ.
In Christ, the eyes of reason are offended, as the eyes of faith
are fed.

Luther made a primary distinction between the *theology of glory* and the *theology of the cross* as two polar ways of thinking about faith. The theology of glory wants to know God in power, wisdom, signs, etc. The theology of the cross recognizes God in suffering, weakness, foolishness, and failure, including death, the natural failure of the flesh. The theology of the cross, that sees God in Christ's suffering, turns then to human suffering and sees Christ there. In a theology of the cross there is a mandate for social service that drives the faithful to be with those who suffer, to advocate for them. The theology of the cross also provides a wide template for the imagination, capacious enough to affirm all features of the world, all aspects of life, even death. It seems to promise that everything one can know or imagine, even the most hopeless events and circumstances, can contain hope. This affirmation is the peculiar mode of communication known in the Christian church as proclamation.

The Christian faith—in the theology of the cross—contains an assurance of freedom to surf on "the waves of what is," with all its risk of wiping out or of losing one's self in the undertow. Rapacious waves may seize and slam not only the surfer, but innocents on the shore as well. Poets attend to these swells of life, to the roiling winds and the glassy sea.

---

1. John Updike, "Stand Fast I Must," in *Hugging the Shore, Essays and Criticism* (New York: Alfred A. Knopf, 1983), 645.

2. Updike, "Stand Fast," 648–49.

3. This will be seen quite clearly in the chapters on Wendell Berry and Scott Cairns.

4. Updike, "Stand Fast," 647–48.

5. This existentially fascinating absence recalls the muse of a poet like R.S. Thomas. Updike refers to the two Thomas poems included in the collection ("The Hand" and "The Porch"), remarking that it would "take a radium counter [to detect the] Christian content" in them, suggesting that Davie might have omitted them in favor of poems of more obvious Christian content by Marianne Moore, Dylan Thomas, E.E. Cummings (and perhaps those of Updike himself?).

6. Richard Wilbur, *New and Collected Poems* (New York: Harcourt Brace & Company, 1989), 233.

7. James Yerkes, ed. John Updike and Religion; *The Sense of the Sacred and the Motions of Grace* (Grand Rapids: William B. Eerdmans Publishing Company, 1999), xiii.

8. Francis of Assisi, "All Creatures of our God and King," tr. William H. Draper.

9. John Updike, *Self-Consciousness: Memoirs* (New York: Alfred Knopf, 1989), 252.

10. Updike, *Self-Consciousness*, 257.

11. 1 Corinthians 13:12.

12. Revelation 21:1.

13. Updike, *Self-Consciousness*, 229. This surfing theme will reappear in the chapter on Mark Jarman, a California surfer.

14. See Paul Althaus, *The Theology of Martin Luther* (Philadelphia: Fortress Press, 1966), especially Chapter 5.

Chapter  2

Faith is the evidence of things not seen.

Hebrews 11:1

All this was a long time ago, I remember,
And I would do it again, but set down
This set down
This: were we led all that way for Birth or Death?
There was birth, certainly
We had evidence no doubt. I had seen birth and death,
But had thought they were different; this Birth was
Hard and bitter agony for us, like Death, our death.
We returned to our places, these Kingdoms,
But no longer at ease here, in the old dispensation,
With an alien people clutching their gods.
I should be glad of another death.

T. S. Eliot (1888–1965)
"Journey of the Magi"

And death shall have no dominion.
Dead men naked they shall be one
With the man in the wind and the west moon;
When their bones are picked clean and the clean
    bones gone,
They shall have stars at elbow and foot;
Though they go mad they shall be sane,
Though they sink through the sea they shall rise again;
Though lovers be lost love shall not;
And death shall have no dominion.

Dylan Thomas (1914–1953)
"And Death Shall Have No Dominion"

∴ 2 ∴
Death in Recent Poetry

Cultural Attitudes about Death

Scholars who examine human perceptions of death tell us that a culture's attitudes about death change whenever there is a significant change in the nature of work, leisure, religion, or family life. Attitudinal shifts will usually be named as "progress" at the time they occur, but in retrospect they may not be healthy changes, nor will they follow a linear path, as, for instance, progress is understood in scientific fields. Given the many significant changes in medicine and technology, it is hardly surprising that American atittudes toward death have altered greatly in the past two hundred years.

James J. Farrell, in his book *Inventing the American Way of Death*, argues that nineteenth-century religious liberalism combined with certain elements of romanticism and scientific naturalism to remove the sting of death from American life. Somber funeral rites, little changed from those of the medieval church in the *Age of Death*, were replaced by optimistic celebrations of life and of its natural evolution through the stage of death. Liberal Christians spoke of immortality as a natural progression in human evolution. In the broader culture, death was no longer imagined as a pilgrimage to another place, but rather as rest or sleep. As an expression of this new belief, cemeteries were situated in places other than somber churchyards. Specially created parks in scenic, rural settings reinforced an attitude of tranquil contemplation and consolation in the face of death. The first and best-known of these "garden cemeteries," Mt. Auburn Cemetery, was founded in Cambridge, Massachusetts in 1831. Farrell writes,

As the pace of their lives quickened, Americans used ideas and institutions to counterpoint the acceleration of the civilization. The image of sleep and the institution of the rural cemetery served the same purpose. Both assured Americans that the sleep of death followed the strenuous life and preceded a restful resurrection. And both made the experiences of death and burial seem more natural.[1]

Farrell observes that as ways of life change over time, our society continues to invent "ways of death."

Contemporary Ways of Death

The Canadian theologian Douglas John Hall writes that people of the present time are not well equipped to "accept or articulate their own personal suffering." He observes:

Some of us are old enough to remember when death was still called "death", when funerals were held in people's parlors, . . . when schoolchildren were caused to read stories and poems in which innocent maidens were drowned and lovers (like Evangeline and Gabriel) did not walk off into the sunset.[2]

To Hall, our inability to face suffering and death makes us unable to enter imaginatively into the suffering of others and drives us to find an enemy, such as an evil nation or person to hate, or a scapegoat, such as a caregiver, to blame. When we become able to acknowledge human suffering and death, we may minister to one another by speaking words that will articulate the emotion of fear and the pain of loss. Poems may serve by supplying the words to interpret and reflect how death feels to the rest of us.

T. S. Eliot once observed that the business of poets is to express the greatest emotional intensity of their time, based upon whatever their time happens to think. Eliot added, as a word of caution, that while poetry may reflect intense human emotions, it does not substitute for philosophy or theology or religion. Assuming that Eliot is right, it would follow that the best poets are not programmed to inspire action or to manipulate opinion. As artists, they work unconstrained by effects and results. This freedom sometimes makes artists a threat to political tyrants as well as to ideological tyrannies. As a doctrine of hope, it is to be affirmed that in the imaginative creative process, artists have access to some of the deeper recesses of human life.

Eliot's comments raise several questions to be considered:
- What is the level and quality of emotional intensity surrounding the thought of death at the beginning of the twenty-first century?
- What emotions—even culturally suppressed emotions, erupting in words—animate the poems that refer to death or otherwise reflect death?
- What images now veil the thought of death?
- What meaning or absence of meaning is joined to death?

Poets have a peculiar potential for innocently drawing out forgotten pieces of the puzzle of our experience. Old wisdom and ancient practices—cultural detritus discounted by the social scientists and other observers of the current scene— might still have relevance within poetry, might still speak to our common human circumstances. Before turning to the lines of emotion, thought, and sound laid around death by five contemporary poets, there are two more questions to discuss:
- What have others noted as the relationship of death to poetry in poetry in our time?
- What makes a contemporary poem about death a religious poem?

Observations on Death in Recent Poetry

Annie Dillard attaches to one of her poems this quotation from the preface to Henry James's 1902 novel, *The Wings of the Dove:* "The poet essentially can't be concerned with the act of dying." Dillard's poem disagrees with its own epigraph as it records the actual last words of the dying. The composition is frantic, sparking, and jittering like a severed live wire, reading in part:

Do you know the Lord's Prayer? Cover me.
Shut the door. Can't see you any more.

I must go home. I am very forlorn at the present
Moment, and I wish I was at Malvern.[3]

After any other life experience one may look back and
reflect upon the experience. Perhaps poets, as reflective artists,
cannot be concerned with their own death because they cannot
get around the event and reflect upon it from the other side.
However, if poetry contains invention in addition to artistic
reflection on past events, then death might be present in the
poet's creations, because death is present in the language.

In fact, poets can be and are concerned with the act of
dying.[4] They are concerned not only with the act of dying but
with the thought of death, with the meaning of death, with the
fear of death, with courage in the face of death, with the indig-
nity of dying, with the final solemnity of death, and with humor
discovered in communicating about death.

Ours is not a day of preoccupation with actual death. We are
entertained by fictional death on the three screens that reflect
our lives: movie, television, and computer. We are excited and
fascinated by death as the end of a video game or the beginning
of a movie thriller, but we no longer romanticize death in lyric
and elegy as, for example, our Victorian ancestors did, or as
Emily Dickinson, a descendant of the Puritans, did with digni-
fied pace and exquisite mournfulness:

Because I could not stop for Death,
He kindly stopped for me;
The carriage held but just ourselves
And immortality.

We slowly drove, he knew no haste,
And I had put away
My labor, and my leisure too,
For his civility.[5]

as well as

I measure every grief I meet
    With analytic eyes;
I wonder if it weighs like mine,
    Or has an easier size.[6]

Compare the tone of Dickinson's compositions with that of an antic poem by David Craig, a contemporary writer:

> Your friend, the end, comes every day:
> doorbells and flowers.
> He eats your grass, spackles your chimney.
> Let him. He is your guest.
>
> Invite him to sit on the porch
> to share your melon, spit the seeds.
> Barefoot, the two of you can collect
> the dirt from between your toes,
> use it against yourselves
> become halls of angry voices.[7]

Death appears to contemporary poets not as the stereotypical hooded skeleton with a scythe, nor as Dickinson's old-fashioned gentleman, but more like an eccentric guest, as in this poem by David Citino:

> When death dances in,
> tap-shoes rattling like dice
> on the floor of your room,
> assure him there's been no mistake;
> ask if you may borrow
> his faded straw hat, his grin.
> ask if you may lead
> waltz him out the door.[8]

A similar casual informality characterizes many death poems today.

One need not look very deeply into the canon of literary poetry to discover reflections of death. In his book on the death poems of W. B. Yeats, Jahan Ramazani reminds us that other poets—Edgar Allan Poe, and Rainer Maria Rilke, for example—were obsessed with death. From the eighteenth century onward the literary interest in death intensified, until, in the twentieth century, Wallace Stevens could write, in "Sunday Morning," that

Death is the mother of beauty; hence from her,
Alone, shall come fulfillment to our dreams
And our desires. . .[9]

Summarizing this trend, Ramazani concludes, "from Yeats, Eliot, and Stevens to Lowell, Plath, Hill, and Heaney, death often seems to be the *raison d'etre* of the modern lyric."[10]

In his book on the meaning of death in American poetry,[11] Anthony Libby begins with discussion of three twentieth-century poets of the generation known as the modernists: Wallace Stevens, T. S. Eliot, and William Carlos Williams; and continues with major chapters on later poets: Robert Lowell, Theodore Roethke, Sylvia Plath, Robert Bly, and W. S. Merwin, all of whom may be called death poets. Libby claims that in our post-Christian age the poet plays the role of the priest, and that mystical poetry—in which the poet/priest addresses death—has arisen as the dominant strain of American poetry.

Mystical patterns of a Christian strain can be seen in T. S. Eliot. Darker patterns of mysticism surfaced earlier in Walt Whitman, then later in poets such as W. S. Merwin and Robert Bly. Libby claims that as Christianity declined among twentieth-century poets, the poet/priests replaced the transcendent God of the church with such objects as nature, or with the thought of "sheer undifferentiated flow," or with other gods, shaped by the imagination in forms given by nature:[12]

> . . . the sense of death is fundamental to our [American] poetry; death is the mother of poetry as well as other forms of beauty. And the idea of death is often connected with ideas of mysticism, whether the mysticism of John of the Cross, as in Eliot, or the mysticism of a new and different mythology, as in Stevens. So the sense of death as well as the mystical experience becomes not only the subject but also the condition of poetic creation for a surprising number of central poets in this place and century. . . .[13]

However, what Libby calls orthodox teaching, and insists on separating from the poets' mystical imaginings, need not be seen as a distinct line of inspiration. In other words, one may take Libby's point and still insist that mysticism may contain "orthodox" Christian teaching. Orthodox means "right praise."

Orthodox Christian thought is that which leads to right and proper praise of God and service of one's neighbor. Right and proper praise may be fed by a mystical river of thought.

In his preface to Olivier Clément's book on Christian mysticism, Jean-Claude Barreau declares that mysticism is central to our human nature. Once human beings have satisfied their physical needs, deeper needs assert themselves. These deeper needs are non-rational and supra-rational, in another word, "mystical." Art and religion, Barreau says, flow from this non-rational source. Mysticism, he writes, is "an attitude of existence . . . a way of living at a greater depth."[14]

What Makes a Death Poem a Religious Poem?

Poets whose work resonates to a Christian reading are those who have somehow, even in spite of themselves, tapped Christian sources. What makes a poem ring with even a faint echo of Christian truth is the presence of Christian inspiration in the "soil" from which the poem grows. A stream of Christian thought may flow and be tasted; it need not be purified or analyzed first. Perhaps the poem assumes a community formed by witness to the Christian mystery. Perhaps the paschal mystery of Christ's suffering and death underlies the literary creation. If this is true, then one may argue that the very contemplation of death and darkness might be a component of Christian witness.

A similar insight comes from Martin Luther, who, in his vivid, medieval world view named darkness, doubt, and the devil as veils of God. According to Luther, faith, as light, could exist only within a field of darkness and doubt. Therefore, darkness and faith belong together. The contemplation of death and darkness might be deemed a Christian activity.

Esthetic and devotional judgment is required to discern the faint music of faith "in, with, and under" any given poem. The music of love often calls to the heart of faith in strange ways. What is more, the one bearing religious witness might be an unwitting poet who, like Balaam's donkey, brays in ways unknown to other donkeys.[15] The poet singing a fragment of a song long forgotten still brings that fragment to the ears of those who might, to their delight, recall the rest of the words.

Introducing a volume entitled *Contemporary Religious Poetry*,[16] Paul Ramsey insists that while a certain poem by Roger Hecht[17] contains "not a hint of grace," its memorable facing of death, its "severe meditation on death," qualifies it for a place in a collection of religious poetry. Ramsey argues that death is present in—even central to—the human preoccupation we call religion.

Religion is concerned with first and last things: birth and death are the primal and final facts of human existence. In between, the middle part of human history, and of each individual human story, contains a complex of variables: accidents, social and environmental factors, evolutionary change, heroic achievements, depravity and meanness, tragedies and failures, provisional successes and temporary achievements. Yet, the constant of death ends each story.

Religion provides rituals to regulate a community's response to death. Ritual words and actions support those who attend to the dying and to the bodies of the dead; they comfort the bereaved. Christian theology as well as personal Christian testimony give central place to statements on death transformed.

In making his case for the kind of poetry that counts as religious, Ramsey comments on the poem "Each Day" by Sr. Maura Eichner, a reflection on the experience of attending a dying person, which concludes:

She lets go
of life gently. We

receive from her hands
the victory of belief,

learning the meaning of
our lives from our grief.[18]

Considered only as a literary creation, "Each Day" is a tender discourse, laid on the page in unexpected and attractive lines, but it has little lift or jolt of metaphor and no transport of image. However, considered as a religious reflection, its final two lines offer an insight almost deep enough to summarize the impetus for this book. The wisdom that we "learn the meaning of our life from our grief" is gained not through thinking about the meaning of death but by engaging in those activities known in Christian circles as ministry: comforting the sick, standing by at the moment of death, encouraging the bereaved, etc.

Compare a poem of similar scope, "In the Nursing Home," by Jane Kenyon. Created out of the observation of a loved one's life situation, the poem invokes God in the face of death. In contrast to the passive and reflective poem above, "In the Nursing Home" actively beseeches on behalf of another:

She is like a horse grazing
a hill pasture that someone makes
smaller by coming every night
to pull the fences in and in.

She has stopped running wide loops,
Stopped even the tight circles.
She drops her head to feed: grass
is dust, and the creekbed's dry.

Master, come with your light
halter. Come and bring her in.[19]

Kenyon gives us a petition from a prayer, turned over by her creative imagination and shaped into a small but fully imagined moving picture. The pastoral image draws the reader's thoughts to a horse—arguably the second most noble creature of earth—and joins a human death to an image of care and connection that had not occurred to us.

A Common Life and A Common Death

One general observation may be made concerning the works under discussion: each of the poets sets his individual response to death within the framework of a larger community. Each observes and reports human communion and connection, even acts of self-giving love. To create poetic texts shaped from the ground of the earth and from the facts of death may be to walk a spiritually healthy path, following Lazarus' friend who marched right up to a cave, thick with the stench of death, and called to life: "Come out!"[20]

Death draws people together. The church understands baptism as a "death" that unites the faithful in community. Out of this death comes life, in the order of grace. Paul wrote to the

Christians in Rome, "we have been united with him in a death like his."[21]

Ezra Pound could not quite fathom why death meant so much to Christians. He wrote:

> And I, "But this beats me,
> Beats me, I mean that I do not understand it;
> This love of death that is in them."[22]

Death means so much to Christians because the life of Jesus runs to the cross and to the tomb, and Christians follow him there. The three-part tribal call of faith begins with a full-voiced cry of mortal pain: *Christ has died!* The other two parts follow in quick succession, as inseparable as the modulation of a wild bird's song: *Christ is risen! Christ will come again!* As birds flock to their gathering ground upon hearing their native call, so in this characteristic call Christians hear the native sound of our human home and assemble to give praise. Various poets gather there too, on the perimeter of things, in the back pew. In the energy of their art they widen the circle of Christian perceptions.

The next chapters turn attention to the work of five contemporary poets. In their creations, and in the methods of their work, they illustrate Christian perspectives on life and death. Geoffrey Hill's memorializing creations are acts of morality and humility rising from his scholar's sensitivity to words and to the human history contained in them. Scott Cairns's works amount to an artistic search in the dense overgrowth of historical theology for core truths about people and their deepest relationships to one another and to God. Mark Jarman's memories of the Eden of childhood repeat a basic human impulse that draws readers back to the tender sprouts of life, and there, perhaps, to the best parts of themselves. R. S. Thomas's devotions to darkness may be read as courageous, ungilded witnesses to what C. S. Lewis called "this world of shadows." Wendell Berry's writings resonate with his commitment to stand with generations past and generations to come—on the same cherished ground—in a return to ancient patterns of biblical stewardship.

These poets do not assume the roles of preachers or teachers. Each one serves his readers as an eccentric guide, the kind the crowd often abandons. The poets disclose corners of life that are not the main stops on the road. They often speak in curious and oblique ways, in words that might, for a moment, change the pace of our own walk through life. Robert Frost said that poetry is "a momentary stay against confusion." Poets are like singers who ignore the score, like drivers who have gone off the road. Yet these eccentric artists circle back to the essential signposts of our lives, and there make their art out of the powerful, elastic elements of language.

In the work of these poets, readers will note frequent transformations of one thing into its opposite. A scholar becomes a warrior, wielding formerly inert words as lively weapons. A pilgrim wanderer, on a difficult journey, arrives at his destination as a native citizen. A parent turns into a child, while the child becomes the parent. The farmer—the planter—becomes the planted seed. A faithful priest changes into a doubter and accepts ministrations of grace. These existential role reversals may be dissonant to our ears and troublesome to our minds. But as we stumble in the darkness on our own paths between death and life, we may gratefully accept these poets as our guides. As they tap the darkness through their art, they may shed a little light for us.

1. James J. Farrell, *Inventing the American Way of Death 1830–1920* (Philadelphia: Temple University Press, 1980), 99ff.

2. Douglas John Hall, *God and Human Suffering: An Exercise In The Theology of the Cross* (Minneapolis: Augsburg, 1986), 61f.

3. Annie Dillard, *Mornings Like This* (San Francisco: Harper Collins, 1996), 74.

4. It might be said that poets—as poets—cannot easily turn the act of their own dying into art. Although even this might not be impossible.

5. Robert N. Linscott, ed., *Selected Poems & Letters of Emily Dickinson* (New York: Doubleday, 1959), 151.

6. Linscott, 136.

7. David Impastato, ed., *Upholding Mystery, An Anthology of Contemporary Christian Poetry* (New York: Oxford University Press, 1997), 69.

8. Impastato, 52.

9. Wallace Stevens, *The Collected Poems of Wallace Stevens* (New York: Knopf, 1990), 66.

10. Jahan Ramazani, *Yeats and the Poetry of Death* (New Haven: Yale University Press, 1990), 7f.

11. Anthony Libby, *Mythologies of Nothing: Mystical Death in American Poetry 1940–70* (Urbana: University of Illinois Press, 1984).

12. Libby, 5.

13. Libby, 15–16.

14. Olivier Clément, *The Roots of Christian Mysticism* (New York: New City Press, 1993), 7–8.

15. Numbers 22:22ff.

16. Paul Ramsey, ed., *Contemporary Religious Poetry* (Mahwah: Paulist Press, 1987), 3ff.

17. Ramsey, 46.

18. Ramsey, 69.

19. Jane Kenyon, *Otherwise, New and Selected Poems* (Saint Paul: Graywolf Press, 1996), 13.

20. John 11:43.

21. Romans 6:5.

22. Ezra Pound, *Canto 29*.

Chapter 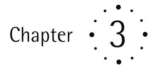 3

. . . the wages of sin is death; but the gift of God is eternal life through Jesus Christ.

Romans 6:23

Lift we then our voices,
   Swell the mighty flood;
Louder still and louder
   Praise the precious blood.

**Italian hymn, 18th century,
tr. Edward Caswall (1814–1878)**

Now the great thing to remember is that all this poetry was once in the language itself, and still underlies the dry bones of even our dictionaries. Every word, a metaphor, perhaps several degrees deep, still has the power to flash meaning back and forth between apparently divergent and intractable planes of being.

Ernest Francisco Fenollosa (1853–1908)

Blood Lines: The Laments of Geoffrey Hill

In a review of Hill's poems, David Yezzi wrote,

> While a growing critical consensus would rank Hill among the greatest living poets in the language, he is also widely considered one of the most difficult in both subject matter and style. Yet despite the cautions inherent in Hill's obscurity and arcane allusiveness . . . [his] is that rare achievement, a profoundly religious poetry.[1]

Hill's poems operate within a moral framework. They aim at being right with respect to the facts, and right with respect to art. If Hill's poems are religious, as Yezzi believes they are, they reflect the severe religion of prophets in the wilderness, and not the faithful praise of singers in the Temple. That is, Hill is not a court poet, writing to please the establishment. (Or, perhaps one might say that he writes on behalf of another, largely invisible establishment: a blessed order of elites, the great religious poets from Milton to Hopkins, Auden, and Eliot.) As an academic, Hill fashions his art out of knowledge, producing dense and knotty creations that do not normally soothe with warm sentiments nor soar with beautiful language. His poems often require the reader to turn to the *Oxford English Dictionary* for assistance. Readers of Hill's poems might be encouraged by T. S. Eliot's comment in an essay on Dante: "Genuine poetry can communicate before it is understood."[2]

If Hill's poems are religious, they do not attempt to inhabit sublime realms nor depict beatific visions. They name and describe the division between what is and what should be. By his own admission, Hill aims not toward the grand or mythical, but the ordinary and experiential. As a literary scholar and a literary artist, Hill looks closely at the nature of words, of thinkers and their thoughts, and sees in these a persistent division between thought and action, and an infused corruption infecting life on earth. We need not read this as pessimism. We might read it as the basis of a Christian world view.

Hill's poems exhibit a careful reading of history in language and an anguished sense of morality. If morality is defined as the perception of the rightness of things, Hill perceives a morality, drawn mainly in violation, from the surface of a broken world and from words that have been drained of their meaning. In Hill's view, not only is the larger world broken and corrupted—in politics, religion, and commerce—but the world of the self is broken as well.

These aspects of perception—of bloodstained history and corrupted tradition on the one hand, and of the poet's own broken self on the other hand—collide within Hill's art. He testifies to the brokenness of the world and of the self through his scrupulous use of language, standing as a prophet-poet, apparently at war with himself and with his art.

In Hill's poetry, the emotional and moral power of words mix with memory in history in ways that do not make for smooth reading. When power, emotions, and memory are not only the subject of the poems but also the tools of the poet and the object of the poet's reflection, reading the poems will not be like reading a newspaper or the latest best-selling novel. Kierkegaard once observed that one should read a book with the same degree of energy and concentration that the author put into writing it. Many of Hill's poems pulse with the energy flowing from their ambiguity of history and language, while being animated with an awareness of the original infection of the heart that ails us all.

Many of Hill's poems refer to death: to the death of ordinary individuals, to the death in war of combatants and of innocents, to the death of words and their meanings in which human history is ingrained. Looking at death through Hill's art raises some themes that will reappear in following chapters. For example, the relationship of death to *place* will be seen in R. S. Thomas and Wendell Berry. Memories of the innocent place of childhood, introduced in this chapter, will be developed in the chapter on Mark Jarman. Reflections on the Hebraic sense of "word," introduced in this chapter, will receive more complete treatment in the chapter on Scott Cairns's poems.

An Artistic Esthetic and a Religious Ethic

Hill sees penitence and humility as disciplines of conscience by which poetry may be created. By extension, through these disciplines life (form) may be brought into conformance with thought (content). The resulting esthetic of poetry may become then the basis for a religious ethic of life. For example, a Christian who submits his life to Jesus as Lord tries to live according to Jesus' words. Then the form of his life—his actions, thoughts, choices, etc.—reflects to some degree the "information" of Christian scripture and tradition. This basic religious principle, according to which action is submitted to belief, may apply to the creation of poems as well. Submitting one's art to the "information" locked inside the history of words implies a kind of reverence. An ethic of literary creation underlies Hill's poems; one might even call it a theology of creation.[3]

William Wordsworth (1770–1850) once defined poetry as "the spontaneous overflow of powerful feelings recollected in tranquility." At first thought, this Romantic[4] statement seems far removed from Hill's intellectually heavy art. Wordsworth's statement sounds as though it could apply to any poem written by anyone wishing to try a little versifying, say, under a shade tree, or more likely at a computer keyboard. Indeed, if one does not care to compare the merits of one composition over against another, it could apply to nearly anyone's best "spontaneous overflow" of feelings or thoughts. Hill works in another way, setting himself apart from Wordsworth's depiction, though perhaps not from Wordsworth's actual method of writing, through scrupulous study and careful—not spontaneous—poetic composition. In a 1980 interview Hill said:

> The poet's true commitment must always be to the vertical richness of language. The poet's gift is to make history and

politics and religion speak for themselves through the
strata of language.[5]

Hill's is a poetry of severe reverence, if reverence is under-
stood as a posture of faith and obedience. His works admit past
and present visions of truth; they encompass hopes and dreams
born through inspiration or revelation outside the shout and
stamp of history and politics. Yet these visions are weighed
down by history, and sometimes stained, even blotted out, by
historical events. The gravity of Hill's poems owes much to his
knowledge and memory. These ingredients make his art seem
heavy and archaic in a culture such as ours, which seems to pre-
fer its literature, as well as its religion, to come packaged in
light and easy forms. His poems model a deep respect for words
and for people. Despite their somber awareness of human
tragedy, one can sometimes detect within them a note of rever-
ent hope.

The Weight of Words

The factual content of Geoffrey Hill's poems comes from his
professional and professorial knowledge of words. It is tempting
for an outsider to imagine Hill's academic community as an
emotionally cool, informed environment where other special-
ists—historians, linguists, etc.—examine language and culture
in their separate but related ways, in adjoining offices. Whether
or not such a picture reflects the academic scene, it is within
academic circles that Hill reads human history through the
history of language.

Words that have remained in a language for generations
gradually acquire their own lineage and history, which may be
traced in the same manner as a human genealogy. It may hap-
pen that a word becomes so misshapen by abuse that it cannot
be restored to useful life. As some words fall out of use, others
are born. Human history reminds us that the power of words has
been used and misused by dictators and tyrants, by advertisers,
by political parties, or by the media, to change the course of his-
tory for good or ill.

Beyond the walls of academia, poets acknowledge a similar
power within words. When Hill-the-professor becomes a poet,
he applies a power of creation to the words he knows so well,

moving beyond discursive scholarship into the creation of living art. Hugh Kenner has written of the dichotomy between Samuel Johnson's and T. S. Eliot's understanding of words; on this point, Hill must be seen as Eliot's intellectual descendant:

> [Samuel] Johnson supposed that words denoted things. A language is simply an assortment of words, and a set of rules for combining them. . . . Eliot felt words as part of that echoing intricacy, Language, which permeates our minds and obeys not the laws of things but its own laws, which has an organism's power to mutate and adapt and survive, and exacts obligations from us because no heritage is more precious.[6]

Hill's artistic method might be expressed in terminology of the mining and metal refining industries: he digs down through history for raw data, and then puts the data under pressure, both intellectual and emotional. Through this creative process he turns the data into a poem, a piece of verbal art. On second thought, pausing at Wordsworth's three terms, "powerful feelings recollected," one might hear a suggestion of the way Hill's poems excavate moments in which history, politics, and religion intersect. These points of intersection are measured with intellectual precision and weighed with moral and artistic sensitivity. Seamus Heaney wrote of Hill,

> There is in Hill . . . [a] hyperconsciousness of words as physical sensations, as sounds to be plumbed, as weights on the tongue. Words in his poetry fall slowly and singly, like molten solder, and accumulate to a dull glowing nub.[7]

Following Heaney, we might say that, as a poet, Hill refines words with the fuel of history and the flame of his own experience and judgment.

The Weight of Sin

The image of a refining fire appears in Malachi, where it will purify the wicked: those who have sinned by ignoring the covenant.[8] We still live in a sin-stained world, where covenant promises are violated, words are broken, and memory fails. "If we say that we have no sin we deceive ourselves, and the truth is not in us."[9] Hill's poems bear consistent witness to brokenness—in the world, in words, and in himself. Perhaps the strongest argument for calling Hill a religious poet may be found in his claim for the atoning work of poetry, as he has written:

> Karl Barth remarked that "sin is the specific gravity of human nature as such." I am suggesting that it is at the heart of this 'heaviness' that poetry must do its atoning work, this heaviness which is simultaneously the 'density' of language and the 'specific gravity of human nature.'[10]

Paul wrote to the Romans that the wages of sin is death.[11] Acutely aware of sin in the lineage of human beings and their words, Hill is a poet of death.

The Weight of the Past

Hill may also be described as a poet of memory, because his poems are replete with memorial dedications and historical memories. He would have us recall and mourn not only the death of other people but also the death of words and their meanings. He stands within the tradition of religious ritual, including Christian liturgy, in which events, laws, promises, and saints are recalled in their rounds, in acts of communal and personal memory. Hill stands also with a small guard of like-minded scouts, watching the horizon of the setting sun and sifting the remnants left by the careless and bloody parade of history. He not only watches and reconstructs meaning for the sake of history, he also observes with regret and distress what has been left behind and lost.

In a review of the second edition of the *Oxford English Dictionary*, Hill mourns the loss of certain uses of words—words coined or given idiosyncratic meaning by such masters as Milton, Bunyan, and Hopkins. He notes that while these archaic definitions are omitted from the OED, some new additions, the word "tofu," for example, are defined at length. Hill asks,

> Is the name of an easily analyzable substance that has appeared on a million menus more real than a word,

peculiarly resistant to analysis, which had lodged itself in a few thousands of minds?[12]

One hopes that Professor Hill has overestimated the number of menus on which the word "tofu" appears. His point is taken, however. Is a word more real because it is part of the current currency of words? Similarly, Hill the moralist would inquire, is a present or a famous life more real than a past or an obscure life? In the economy of God's kingdom—the economy of the spirit—each true life, each fit meaning, is loved and kept.

Poetry and Praise

Part of the renowned difficulty of Hill's poems might result from his apparent personal disregard for approval or praise. He does not write for fame and popular adulation. The only colleagues whose approval he might wish to seek are no longer to be found among the living. These lines that Hugh Kenner wrote about T. S. Eliot could apply to Hill as well:

> [He] invokes some two centuries' philological effort to recover the deepest memories of the tribe. It was with the example of a scholarship committed in that way to finding the immemorial energies of language that he perceived how the most individual parts of a poet's work may be those in which the dead poets, his ancestors, assert their immortality most vigorously, and also how in language used with right attention a network of tentacular roots may reach down to the deepest terrors and desires.[13]

Here the morality of Hill's work comes to light again, as well as his religious point of view. To Hill, praise is not something owed an author. Praise is a religious term; praise is properly directed to God, the Creator, alone. To put this in other theological words, when we are and do what we were created to be, we give praise to God by our very being. Gerard Manley Hopkins implies that any living being—a kingfisher, a dragonfly—by doing what it was created to do, gives a reflected glory:

> Each mortal thing does one thing and the same:
> Deals out that being indoors each one dwells;

Selves—goes its self; myself it speaks and spells,
Crying *What I do is me: for that I came.*[14]

The perennial problem, of course, is that our hearts and our minds do not conform to our actions. Again, as Paul wrote to the Christians in Rome, "for I do not do the good I want, but the evil I do not want is what I do."[15] Hill's poems explicate the first part of Paul's admission and will not allow us to forget the second. As will be seen in the poem "Christmas Trees," praise is a natural outcome of the proper conformity of thought to action. Although Hill does not make this connection explicitly, this conformity, in a word, is *truth,* toward which the poet must strive, and, indeed, toward which a human life is directed. As a moralist and a theologian of praise, Hill stands in the company of religious truth-tellers.

Hill's readers may identify in his poems a high level of factual (historical) content, as well as a high degree of moral and emotional passion from the poet's own life. Added to these are a thorough knowledge of the English literary heritage, as well as a mastery of the technical aspects of poetry—form, meter, line, diction, syntax, etc. Hill brings these "tools" to bear on a creative process that weighs words to a fine degree, and, in so doing, weighs human culture, including its moral and religious aspects. The intellectual and moral "pressure" exerted on the language serves as a kiln of creativity from which emerges an artifact of verbal art: a poem.

Still, as always, the world is full of the darkness of deceit. Processes and systems break down. Infections of thought and false reports mislead us. Memories fail us, and passions blind us. Hill knows that we deceive ourselves and others in many ways. Indeed, an awareness of sin seems to be a common foundation of all the poets considered in this book. Hill is fully aware of the sin of duplicity in human action and motives. He speaks to our condition, as the world is darkened by clouds of hatred leading to death. It should come as no surprise, then, that Hill is also a poet of war.

Images of War

Poet Wilfred Owen, who was killed in action during World War I, wrote:

What passing-bells for these who die as cattle?
—Only the monstrous anger of the guns
Only the stuttering rifles' rapid rattle
Can patter out their hasty orisons.[16]

Owen finds no dignity in the death of these soldiers. Geoffrey Hill follows Owen as a clear-eyed poet of war. When he turns to the blood-red fields of history, his voice rises to a prophetic pitch. War stirs the dark side of human nature. The blood of war and of incessant violence is a fascinating flood, an awesome chaos. His poem "Canaan," from his volume of the same name, begins:

They march at God's
pleasure through Flanders
with machine-pistols,
chorales, cannon
of obese bronze,
with groaning pushcarts,
to topple Baal.[17]

Hill layers words from the conflicts of many centuries. The "march at God's pleasure" recalls Joshua's march into Canaan as well as every other Joshua's march into other promised lands to overthrow the hated infidels. There is ambiguity in every human endeavor.

More than once Hill's poems play on the words *Sheol* and *Shiloh*. *Sheol* is the Hebrew word for the pit of judgment and death, or the abode of the dead. *Shiloh* names two sites on separate continents: in ancient Canaan, a city of the biblical covenant, and in the United States, a Civil War battle in which thousands died on the grounds of a church of that name:

Whose passion was to find out God in this
His natural filth, voyeur of sacrifice, a slow
Bloody unearthing of the God-in-us.
But with what blood, and to what end, Shiloh?[18]

"Dark-Land,"[19] another poem in the volume *Canaan*, conjures up the same ambiguity in describing the current state of the English church, hard-pressed by the world and exposed to the withering elements of culture and history:

> blazed at from rayed clouds,
> rallying to that place,
> Sheol if not Shiloh.

Reading through Hill's poems one notes a progression in sound and visual rhyme from *Sheol* and *Shiloh* to *Siloam* and *Shalom,* and even to the ancient note in the Psalms that calls for a liturgical interlude: *Selah.* The sequence imitates an order of grace: hellfire and war give way to healing and peace, after which comes the call to praise.

The Music of Memory

Hill has grouped some of his poems into cycles and series, with themes that circle and return to unexpected points. The cyclical structure is reminiscent of ritual: repetitive prayers in which the words may vary but the formula remains consistent. The connection with elements of Jewish and Christian liturgy becomes stronger through Hill's frequent addition of memorial names, calling his readers to a repeated remembrance of a shared history.

Hill's poems seem to say that in the course of history too much blood has been shed. The words of sacred ritual—printed carefully in art and in the lifeblood of human culture—have been overwritten with gory gibberish. The valley of death may be found right outside the rear wall of the Temple; mayhem is a close neighbor of *Shalom.* A cyclical movement through history is especially evident in "Ezekiel's Wheel,"[20] a four-part poem which begins:

> Consider now the valley
> of Hinnom—the trucks
> from the abattoir
> skidding their loads,
> the shameless body parts.
> Ezekiel's wheel
> shall encompass all. . . .

The initial image in the poem places us in the valley of Hinnom, south of Jerusalem, which was notorious under Ahaz (mid-eighth to mid-seventh century B.C.) as the scene of the sacrifice of children. Hill overlays this terrible place with words recalling twentieth-century atrocities, interweaving the chronologies of horror from then and now. The result is framed starkly by the righteous absence of God, an emptiness lessened by the faint repetition of Ezekiel's wheel as a refrain, turning over and over with a hint of a midnight harvest:

gleaning to the last
corner of the worst field
the bane of Judah.

In "Ezekiel's Wheel," as well as in many other poems, Hill has written the funeral music for the end of the war-torn twentieth century.

A Prophet of Pain and Hope

Readers who dig beneath the surface of Hill's poems may uncover seeds of hope among the words and lines. For Christians, hope comes through a name, in words, in the Word made flesh, and in memory. Memory and hope join in the poem, "Christmas Trees,"[21] in which Hill remembers Dietrich Bonhoeffer, the German pastor and theologian executed by the Nazis. The poem begins:

Bonhoeffer in his skylit cell
bleached by the flares' candescent fall,
pacing out his own citadel,

restores the broken themes of praise,
encourages our borrowed days,
by logic of his sacrifice.

A Christmas tree carries the weight of memory, emotion, and symbol. In the dead of winter when other trees lie dormant, it remains green. An inhabitant of the wild forest, it is brought into the house. A natural wonder, it is then gilded by human hands, so that it defies both the darkness of winter and the danger of the woods by its lights and decorations. For many people it recalls childhood, when generations no longer with us were alive, surrounding us with their love. A Christmas tree in full glory stands as an annual emotion-filled symbol of hope.

Within his poem, Hill invites the reader to see the shape of Bonhoeffer's imprisonment as hope in a dark world. The ornament that is lighted on this Christmas tree is Bonhoeffer himself. His life of integrity, his witness to the Christian gospel through his words and his actions, spoke a true word of hope—in his martyrdom—to a world imprisoned in sin and evil. The real, meaningful word is spoken in the action of a human life. An act of love, Hill knows, is an act of sacrifice, a turning to another person, or a turning to God in service and love.

This is my commandment, that you love one another as I have loved you. Greater love has no man than this, that a man lay down his life for his friends.[22]

The line "by logic of his sacrifice" implies a final conformation of belief and action. Bonhoeffer died for what he believed.

Hill has written that the poet's true task is to work within an aesthetic of atonement—at-one-ment—bringing individual words into conformity with the overall shape of things, bringing thought and life together. The poet labors to square a general belief with a specific action. He writes,

I would suggest . . . that the proof of a poet's craft is precisely the ability to affect an at-one-ment between the 'local vividness' and the 'overall shape', and that is his truth telling. When the poem 'comes right with a click like a closing box', what is there effected is the atonement of aesthetics with rectitude of judgment.[23]

One might say, following Hill, that, with brutal finality, Bonhoeffer's martyr's death was a life coming "right with a click like a closing box."

Hill has never flinched from grappling with the hottest, most painful moments in history. Through his memorializing, though, he supplies a balm of ritual remembrance to cool overheated memory. A sense of sun and heat is intensified by the visual depiction on the cover of his volume, *Canaan*. It shows a chaotic image of a boxy village afloat in a distorted jumble on the waves of a rolling flood. A line of stylized suns beats down on the black-and-red scene. This drawing, combined with the title of the collection, calls to mind some latter-day Beth-shemesh,[24] a city dedicated to praise of the sun god. Throughout the prophetic books of the Hebrew Bible, prophet after prophet decried pagan idolatry and preached a return to worship of the one true God. One such lament against idolatry is recorded in Ezekiel 8:

> And he brought me into the inner court of the house of the Lord; there, at the entrance of the temple of the Lord, between the porch and the altar, were about twenty-five men, with their backs to the temple of the Lord, and their faces toward the east. Then he said to me, 'Have you seen this, O mortal? Is it not bad enough that the house of Judah commits the abominations done here? Must they fill the land with violence, and provoke my anger still further? See, they are putting the branch to their nose! Therefore I will act in wrath; my eye will not spare, nor will I have pity; and though they cry in my hearing with a loud voice, I will not listen to them.'[25]

Lamentations

Although many of Hill's poems work over and around Christian themes, their tone is predominantly pre-Christian. They ring with wild war music, proclaiming a prophet's pain and offering a seer's dark vision. They utter mournful music, too, acknowledging personal and corporate sin. In both respects they stand with the book of Lamentations, being grounded in an awareness of history stained in violence. The verses within Lamentations constitute a communal songbook mourning the Lord's abandonment of Jerusalem and its people at the time of the city's destruction by the Babylonians in 587 B.C.:

> Jerusalem sinned grievously, so she has become a mockery;
> all who honored her despise her, for they have seen her
>   nakedness;
> she herself groans, and turns her face away.[26]

Following the memorial dedication and preceding the table of contents of his collection *Canaan*, Hill sets out texts from the Geneva Bible of 1560, stitching together portions from Judges 3, Psalm 106, and Zephaniah 2. The conglomerate passage has a strange liquid sound and appearance, as if the old English words of divine condemnation were themselves a wave of judgment, drowning sinful humanity. Bruce Metzger writes that while

> the Geneva Bible was never authorized, it became at once the people's book, the household Bible of the English-speaking nations, and it held this place for three quarters of a century. It was the Bible used by Shakespeare and John Bunyan, and it was the Bible of the Puritans who settled New England.[27]

One sees in the cover illustration of *Canaan*, and hears in the opening passage, prophetic judgment on a nation and on its church, its spiritual center, both of which seem to have lost their way and their words, their promised shelter and safety:

> ... very late he saw it
> at Dedham: the English
> church as it must be
> charred in its own standing,
>
> small, distinct, monochrome. ....[28]

Still, the reader is warmed by the occasional line that draws memory and hope together in strange and beautiful reverence, as in "Of Coming Into Being and Passing Away,"[29] the final lines of which are:

> but by occasion
> visions of truth or dreams
> as they arise—
>   to terms of grace
> where grace has surprised us—
> the unsustaining
>   wondrously sustained

The surprising grace that Hill praises cannot hold off the returning darkness or free us from the limitations of old age. The fruits of that grace, even if not acknowledged, sustain human life in the world.

Even at the points where Hill's works contain stronger Christian overtones, the Christianity they espouse is not full-voiced praise given to a resurrected Jesus. Their experience includes crucifixion and burial, but not resurrection. In the words of the Apostles' Creed, Hill's poems assent to the second article of belief in Jesus Christ, that he

Suffered under Pontius Pilate,
Was crucified, died, and was buried.
  He descended into hell.

But they do not continue beyond that to the third day: "On the third day he rose again." Pondering this, the words "restraint" and "reserve" come to mind, to be added to "reverence," in describing Hill's poems. In some sense, restraint and reserve allow the living processes of repeated ritual to effect healing within communities. Rituals carry meaning much greater than words can describe. As a poet attuned to the history and meaning of words within culture, Hill works over the material of human culture, being content, as well, to let God have God's own word.

As Hill's poems characteristically refrain from contemplation of the creed's "third day" they also refrain from Genesis' seventh-day rest. Hill's early and well-known poem "Genesis"[30] ends with creation's sixth day, admitting no hallowed sabbath. As in many of Hill's poems, the scene is constructed of scripture, tradition, history, ritual, and song. The final stanza pairs a gruesome, bone-crushing view of human history with a rare explicit notation of redemption's location, concluding with a barely perceptive hope:

On the sixth day, as I rode
In haste about the works of God,
With spurs I plucked the horse's blood.

By blood we live, the hot, the cold,
To ravage and redeem the world:

There is no bloodless myth will hold.

And by Christ's blood are men made free
Though in close shrouds their bodies lie
Under the rough pelt of the sea;

Though Earth has rolled beneath her weight
The bones that cannot bear the light.

Hill's poems might be heard as a restraint on our human tendency toward idolatry, including the typical American enthusiasm for greeting celebrities and spectacles with indiscriminate and misplaced praise. Christian readers might also recognize in his works a warning against the classical errors of the Christian spirit, such as romanticism, pantheism, transcendentalism, or Pelagianism. In other words, Hill's poems seem to imply orthodox Christian teaching. In the indirect way of art, they admonish us to avoid arm-raising, feel-good religion. Equally, they warn against unreligious ideologies that glory too much in the power of the world or soar on human acheievement to self-destruction in the heat of the burning sun.

The World's Lifeblood

For Hill, the poet's creative art always involves a measure of sacrifice. Throughout his poems, images of blood, claws, words, and birds may be seen as references to ink, pen, words, and messengers. The lines of the second stanza of "Genesis" imagine a compelling scene:

The second day I stood and saw
The osprey plunge with triggered claw,
Feathering blood along the shore,
To lay the living sinew bare.

One is reminded of Gerard Manley Hopkins's kingfisher, appearing as a winged, flashing messenger over the water, on fire with the indwelling glory of God ("as kingfishers catch fire, dragonflies draw flame"), but Hill's osprey is a war bird, with sharp claws for drawing sacrificial blood. The blood drizzling on the dry land resembles the bird's own feathers. This bird, this creator, this poet, writes *itself* in the sand.

Words have clawed at Hill throughout his life as he has contemplated the ambiguity of language and the tragic history of humankind, and has faced memories of his own life. Words have "drawn blood" in vicious, calculated—and of course painful—ways. A moving death poem, "The Stone Man,"[31] recalls the poet's father, who was a constable in Bromsgrove, and describes an early and painful call to a difficult and treacherous vocation in the service of words:

Recall, now, the omens of childhood:
The nettle-clump and rank elder-tree;
The stones waiting in the mason's yard:

Half-recognized kingdom of the dead:
A deeper landscape lit by distant
Flashings from their journey. At nightfall

My father scuffed clay into the house.
He set his boots on the bleak iron
Of the hearth; ate, drank, unbuckled, slept.

I leaned to the lamp; the pallid moths
Clipped its glass, made an autumnal sound.
Words clawed my mind as though they had smelt

Revelation's flesh. . . .

The images of the distantly lit gravestone and the moth at the lamp recall Ezekiel's vision[32] in which "living creatures darted to and fro, like a flash of lightning." Above this strange scene, the voice of the Lord God gives words to the prophet:

He spread it before me; it had writing on the front and on the back, and written on it were words of lamentation and mourning and woe. He said to me, O mortal, eat what is offered to you; eat this scroll, and go, speak. . . .

Prophet and Priest

Frequent instances of prophetic utterance and prophetic judgment have been noted in Hill's work. In addition to fulfilling the role of a prophet, Hill's poetic vocation includes fulfilling the role of priest as well. By blood he has been called into an artistic sacramental ministry. He handles the blood of other people, interprets the world through it, speaks to it, lets it run through his fingers, and sometimes proclaims his disgust at being possessed by such a calling. In "Three Baroque Meditations"[33] he ends the first meditation:

> I confess to the priest in me;
>
> I am shadowed by the wise bird
> Of necessity, the lithe
> Paradigm Sleep-and-Kill.

Hill's persistent memorializing also fills a priestly function. His memorials are not eulogies. Rather, they ritualize the remembrance of persons in his life in such a way that the ordinary events of an individual life are turned into art. Remembering other people who have died, including the famous, such as Bonhoeffer, but especially those closest to us, is a devotion recommended by Hill's poems. Through his literary sacramentalism, Hill testifies to the ultimate value of human lives.

In his preface to Hill's volume *Somewhere is Such a Kingdom*, Harold Bloom writes of the power and the despair of Hill's poetry. He comments that Hill is a poet of the *Word*

> in the Hebraic sense of *dahvar,* a word that is also an act,
> a bringing forward of something previously held back in
> the self.[34]

Within the Judeo-Christian tradition God's word is God, and God's word is true. Similarly, our words *are* ourselves, but often our words are not true. A careful poet's word gives voice to the poet's very self, sometimes painfully, as a *word*. Though Hill may appear to be a poet of the intellect, he can still declare:

. . . poetic utterance is nonetheless an utterance of the self,
the self demanding to be loved, demanding love in the
form of recognition and 'absolution.'[35]

According to Hill, love recognizes the beloved and offers for-
giveness. A sense of the bonds of love may be seen throughout
Hill's poems.

Memorials to Love

The term *parentalia* originated in ancient Rome, where it
described periodic rituals held in honor of dead parents or rela-
tives. Hill has appropriated the archaic term to apply it to two
poems in *Canaan*.

When Isaiah announces the salvation of God's love, he
recalls the genealogy of faith:

But you, Israel, my servant, Jacob, whom I have chosen, the
offspring of Abraham, my friend . . . do not fear, for I am
with you.[36]

When the poet/priest calls readers to remember the sources
of love, he retraces familial bloodlines. Our lifeblood is the
blood of our parents and ancestors, as well as the blood of our
brothers and sisters. Standing in an ancestral line, with a
genealogy behind us, we carry the history of our parents with us.
In the Christian sacrament we are joined to others through the
body and blood of Jesus. Memory connects us to families and
loved ones in a similar way.

The first "Parentalia"[37] begins:

The here-and-now finds vigil transfiguring
whatever is
    yet ignorant of your beauty.
Any one of us, given a certain light,
    shall make and be immortal. . .

The next line draws our attention to the heavenly Jerusalem,
the place of Christian hope, the home of God's people, and the
location of Jesus' sacrifice of love for the forgiveness of the

world. The last line of the first Parentalia might be preceded by this gloss: other than through considerable honoring of other people, especially those dearest to us,

I cannot tell how we might be otherwise
drawn to the things occluded, manifold,
the measureless that stands
                    even so depleted
in the faint rasp of dry autumnal flowers.

The final adjective recalls the "autumnal sound" made by the moth on the lamp in "The Stone Man," a poem written more than thirty years before "Parentalia."

When we stand in the autumn of our lives we may no longer postpone thoughts of our own mortality. When our parents have died, and we stand as the oldest living generation, we carry our parents' love for us in our memories and, in turn, offer our love to the next generation. In these rounds of autumnal remembering, there is an artistic and moral method for Hill, the priest/poet.

The second "Parentalia"[38] bears a further inscription, a reference to Daniel 12:3–4, 9, which reads,

Those who are wise shall shine like the brightness of the sky, and those who lead many to righteousness, like the stars forever and ever and ever. But you, Daniel, keep the words secret and the book sealed until the time of the end. Many shall be running back and forth, and evil shall increase. . . . He said, 'Go your way, Daniel, for the words are to remain secret and sealed until the time of the end. . . .'

The tone of the poem is typical of Hill's theology: coiled and compressed with the power of language and bowed in reverence to history. There can be, and indeed there is, instruction without full knowledge. There can be representation and encouragement without complete understanding. Even with one's mind fully equipped, and one's senses alert, things of earth and heaven still are seen through Paul's opaque glass. "Parentalia"[39] are among Hill's poems that show where we might look for strength in the course of our lives.

As a prayer from the liturgy of the burial of the dead says, "the generations rise and pass away before you."[40] Each generation needs words from the past generation to help them on their way. For some, those words resound as a blessing of encouragement and a release from the fear of death:

> But go, as instrumental, of the Lord,
>   life-bound to his foreknowledge
> and in his absence making your return
> to the generations, the rosaceae,
> the things of earth snagging the things of grace. . .[41]

A field of blood-red roses, blooming and then dying away to make room for the next field, stands for an order of grace and of sacrificial love passed on through the generations. Human beings are born and grow up in the light of the history of their ancestors. They inherit their ancestors' words and then leave those words behind them when they die, transmuted into new cultural, scientific, and political features. Generations follow generations in processions of life on earth. In careful use of language, lessons of love may be recalled and relearned.

1. David Yezzi, "The Poet's Duty of Opacity," in *Commonweal*, November 7, 1997.

2. See T. S. Eliot, *Dante* (London: Faber & Faber, 1929).

3. See Hill's essay, "Poetry as 'Menace' and 'Atonement," in *The Lords of Limit* (New York: Oxford University Press, 1984).

4. Romanticism, as a movement, flourished from the end of the eighteenth century through the first half of the nineteenth century. It was characterized by innovation in poetic form and was concerned with nature and subjective emotion. The interests of Romanticism—or of any other literary movement—have never entirely disappeared. Robert Pinsky has argued that all contemporary poetry is traditional, in that it trades on what has gone before. The effort that would be required to supplant all past tradition with something entirely new would be neither worthwhile nor desirable.

5. Quoted in Avril Horner, "The Poet's True Commitment," in Gregory Salyer et al., ed., *Literature and Theology at Century's End* (Atlanta: Scholars Press, 1995), 159.

6. Hugh Kenner, *The Pound Era* (Berkeley, University of California Press, 1971), 123.

7. Seamus Heaney, *Preoccupations: Selected Prose 1968–1978* (New York: Farrar, Straus and Giroux, 1980), 106.

8. Malachi 3:1–4.

9. 1 John 1:8.

10. Geoffrey Hill, *The Lords of Limit, Essays on Literature and Ideas* (New York: Oxford University Press, 1984), 15.

11. Romans 6:23.

12. *Times Literary Supplement,* April, 1989.

13. Kenner, *The Pound Era,* 110.

14. Catherine Phillips, ed., *Gerard Manley Hopkins, A Critical Edition of the Major Works* (New York: Oxford University Press, 1986), 129.

15. Romans 7:19.

16. Wilfred Owen, "Anthem for Doomed Youth." An orison is a prayer.

17. Geoffrey Hill, *Canaan* (New York: Houghton Mifflin, 1997), 10. The OED indicates that *flander* is an orange color as well as an orange-colored brick. Hill's poetic excavations often come back to rocks and stones.

18. Geoffrey Hill, *Somewhere is Such a Kingdom* (Boston: Houghton Mifflin, 1975), 55.

19. Hill, *Canaan,* 54.

20. Hill, *Canaan,* 56–59.

21. Geoffrey Hill, *New and Collected Poems* (New York: Houghton Mifflin, 2000), 159.

22. John 15:12–13 (RSV).

23. Hill, *Lords of Limit,* 10.

24. According to *Harper's Bible Dictionary* (San Francisco: Harper and Row, 1985) there were four cities noted in biblical and extra-biblical sources that bore the name of Beth-shemesh. All four seem to have been centers for a sun cult.

25. Ezekiel 8:16–18.

26. Lamentations 1:8.

27. "English Versions of the Bible" in *The New Oxford Annotated Bible, New Revised Standard Version* (New York: Oxford University Press, 1991), 402.

28. Hill, *Canaan,* 54.

29. Hill, *Canaan,* 4.

30. Hill, *Somewhere is Such a Kingdom,* 3–5.

31. Hill, *Somewhere is Such a Kingdom,* 75.

32. See Ezekiel 1–3.

33. Hill, *Somewhere is Such a Kingdom*, 79.

34. Hill, *Somewhere is Such a Kingdom*, xix. This idea is discussed more fully in connection with Scott Cairns; see page 73ff.

35. Hill, *The Lords of Limit*, 17.

36. Isaiah 41:8–9.

37. Hill, *Canaan*, 28.

38. Hill, *Canaan*, 41.

39. 1 Corinthians 13:12.

40. *Lutheran Book of Worship*, 210.

41. Hill, *Canaan*, 41.

Chapter 4

For I know that my Redeemer lives,
and that at the last he will stand upon the earth;
And after my skin has been thus destroyed,
then in my flesh I shall see God,
Whom I shall see on my side,
and my eyes shall behold, and not another.

Job 19:25–27

See the God blasphem'd and doubted
In the schools of Greece and Rome;
See the pow'rs of darkness routed,
Taken at their utmost gloom.

God all-bounteous, all-creative
Whom no ills from good dissuade,
Is incarnate, and a native
Of the very world he made.

Christopher Smart (1722–1771)
*Hymns and Spiritual Songs for the Fasts and Festivals
of the Church of England*

Perplexed in faith, but pure in deeds,
At last he beat his music out.
There lives more faith in honest doubt,
Believe me, than in half the creeds.

He fought his doubts and gathered strength,
He would not make his judgement blind,
He faced the specters of the mind
And laid them: thus he came at length

To find a stronger faith his own;
And Power was with him in the night,

Which makes the darkness and the light,
And dwells not in the light alone,

But in the darkness and the cloud,
As over Sinai's peaks of old,
While Israel made their gods of gold,
Although the trumpet blew so loud.

Alfred, Lord Tennyson (1809–1892)
In Memoriam XCV

· 4 ·
The Taste of Death: Scott Cairns

The initial poem in Scott Cairns's collection *Recovered Body*[1]
bears the evocative title "Necropolitan." The wordplay denotes
both an imagined city of death and an unusual name for a fla-
vor of ice cream. This strange and wonderfully sweet ice cream
is being tasted on the streets of a foreign yet familiar city that
pulses with the remembrance of the blessed dead on All Souls'
Day, or *Dia de los Muertos:*

> Not your ordinary ice cream, though the glaze
> of these skeletal figures affects
> the disposition of those grinning candies
> one finds in Mexico, say, at the start of November,
> though here, each face is troublingly familiar,
> exhibits the style adopted just as one declines
> any further style—nectar one sips just as he
> draws his last, dispassionate breath, becomes
> citizen of a less earnest electorate. One learns
> in that city finally how to enjoy a confection,
> even if a genuine taste for this circumstance
> has yet to be acquired, even if it is oneself
> whose sugars and oils now avail a composure
> which promises never to end, nor to alter.

The poem speaks of and to the senses, while referring both to
religious rituals and spiritual ideas. Cairns places "Necropolitan"
as an introduction, before the first titled division of his poems,
in order to announce his theological standpoint: he is a poet of
death. Cairns takes his stand, with his art, on sacred literary
ground where he maintains a Christian stance while being influ-

enced by biblical patterns of thought and belief within the Hebrew scriptures.

This chapter will analyze the theology of the word contained in several of Cairns's poems, showing how that theology can be opened up to a more general discussion of the power of words, with implications for the crafting of a poem and the ordering of a Christian life.

A Jewish World View

Cairns's Hebraic strand of thought may be clarified by comparing the teaching of Abraham Heschel, a Jewish scholar whose literary and moral authority is acknowledged well beyond Jewish circles. Though a meticulous scholar, Heschel writes with broad passionate strokes rather than with scholarly restraint. His books energetically call their readers' attention to the religious milieu of the Hebrew prophets while showing his broad outlook on life. He writes:

> If life is sensed as surprise, as a gift, defying explanation, then death ceases to be a radical, absolute negation of what life stands for. For both life and death are aspects of a greater mystery, the mystery of being, the mystery of creation. Over and above the preciousness of particular existence stands the marvel of its being related to the infinite mystery of being or creation.[2]

Within Heschel's world view, the body—our own mystery— is a good creation, formed from the good earth. Death, when it claims the body, plays its rightful part in the earth-mystery of life. Cairns, a Christian, would agree with Heschel in defending the unity of life and death in the mystery of creation.

Gnosticism

Cairns also affirms another, similar unity: that of body and spirit. In so doing, he refutes *gnosticism*, which has plagued Christian thought since the first centuries with its temptation to deny the material world. Historians of philosophy use the term gnosticism for a number of related theological viruses that arose on the western side of the Mediterranean Sea and infected the early church. Tracing its development, Bengt Hagglund describes a "religious potpourri in which Christianity and Greek philosophy are blended together."[3]

In addition to teaching a basic dualism between the world of the spirit and the material world, gnosticism carried theological, intellectual, and ethical implications:

Theological: there are two Gods, a higher God of the spiritual realm who has nothing to do with the lower realm, and a lower God who created the world.

Intellectual: Salvation is available through special insight or knowledge (*gnosis*) in the form of mystery-wisdom. This knowledge exists on a more exalted level than the level of faith.

Ethical: The material world, including the body, is inherently evil and needs to be overcome through salvific release of the soul from the material world.

Hagglund writes,

> The suffering and death of Christ was of no importance to Gnosticism; what He did to enlighten men, on the other hand, was emphasized to the exclusion of all else. He was the conveyor of that knowledge which man needs in order to be able to launch forth on the journey back to the higher world of light . . . . Gnosticism wanted to transform Christianity into a mythological speculation. Its doctrine of salvation implied a denial of that which is most essential to the Christian faith. The simple faith of Christianity was to be superseded by the higher knowledge of the Gnostics, which took the form of a personal conviction concerning the realities of the spiritual world. . . . Gnostics also denied the resurrection of the body, on the basis of the idea that everything physical or material is evil.[4]

Cairns joins a long line of thinkers who have defended the faith against the gnostic tendency to deny the body and to look outside the facts of physical existence for spiritual insight. Hearing the sometimes polemical heat infused in Cairns's work leads one to believe that gnostic ideas still infect Christian thought. In isolating and examining the problem, Cairns employs a dialectical pair of terms: the Hebrew *davar*[5] and the Greek *Logos*, both of which may be translated into English as *word*.

At stake for Cairns in the *davar/Logos* dichotomy are two different views of the power of words, and therefore two divergent philosophies of the moment when words shall cease, that is, two opposing views of human life and death. Cairns attaches considerable importance to the division on this issue within Christian thought. In his poem "In Lieu of Logos" he indicates the intellectual dimensions of the problem:

Let's suppose some figure more Hebraic
in its promise, more inclined to move

from one provisional encampment
to the next, then discover the effect

wandering tenders even as it draws
the weary hiker on to further

speculation, crossing what has seemed so
like barren country but whose very

barrenness proves a prod for yet another
likely story. The old Jews liked *davar,*

which did something more than just point fingers
to what lies back behind one's fussy, Greek

ontology of diminishing
returns. I have come to like it too, *word*

with a future as dense as its past,
a *Ding Gedicht* whose chubby letters each

afford a pause at which the traveler
rubs his chin and looking up entertains

a series of alternate routes, just now
staying put at the borrowed outpost,

but marveling how each turn of the head
gives way to distance, layers every term

of travel—each terminal—with reprieve,
invites indeterminate, obscure enormity

to gather at the glib horizon's edge.[6]

In choosing to create a poem containing an insightful and
undisguised theological argument against the gnosticisms he
has known, Cairns shows the sophistication of his theology and
perhaps also the maturity of his religious feeling. Clearly, Cairns
has studied the meaning of theological language, its power, and
the ways that power may be misused. He is not, in this poem at
least, fishing in a murky spiritual sea for a tug of felt insight. His
theological proposal is worthy of a theological analysis and
response.

Unlike images, for example, theological arguments are not
often loaded into poems. Such arguments are more likely to be
found within the pages of scripture or in creeds, and in the writ-
ings that respond to them, such as sermons and hymns.
Receptive listeners may enjoy the satisfying way in which the-
ological arguments neatly organize their thoughts and feelings.
Yet, such arguments may also deaden the lively word. In the
service of certain literalisms and fundamentalisms, they remove
their hearers from the disorder of earth and the disappoint-
ments of life, setting them in an artificial kingdom where mer-
ciful deeds and the confession of ambiguous truths remain
packed away beneath plastic ideals of faith. In consequence,
faith becomes over-intellectualized, a condition to which theo-
logical students are prone, and a danger against which Cairns
would be viligant.

A brief review of the concepts and principles carried within
the Hebrew *davar* on one hand, and in the Greek *Logos* on the
other, in the early church and later in Jewish thought and
Christian theology, will show why Cairns, as a Christian poet,
promotes what he sees as the connotations of *davar* over those
of *Logos*.

Davar versus Logos

One must assume that the *Logos* Cairns has in mind is the
one known in the prologue of John's Gospel:

In the beginning was the word (Logos), and the word was
with God and the word was God.

The fullest streams of meaning flowing into this *Logos* are
indeed ancient tributaries from Greek thought. Rene Girard
has said that "the presence of [the *Logos*,] more than any other
factor, has long led to this text being regarded as the most
'Greek' of the four Gospels."[7] If the Greek origin of the *Logos*
principle is accepted, then the antecedents of the Christian
gospel are not only the patriarchs and the Hebrew prophets—
their feet planted in the ancient Near Eastern crucible of the
biblical narrative—but Greek philosophers as well. In Cairns's
mind, *Logos* seems to stand for philosophical notions of reason,
thought, agency, and plan, brought from an outside source to
bear on the biblical story. (Ancient academies of learning were
the sources of these unsettling foreign ideas.) Cairns and others
in his camp would rather read the Bible as an ambiguous, con-
tradictory, suggestive, original human story; in other words, as a
humanly complex but simply narrated epic.

Hellenistic Judaism (as distinct from Palestinian Judaism)
flourished in the Egyptian city of Alexandria in the first
Christian century. There, urban Jewish thinkers such as Philo
allowed philosophical ideas to fertilize their religious thought.
To Philo, the *Logos* was the intermediary between God and the
universe. He wrote that the *Logos* is "God's agent in history and
the means by which the mind apprehends God."[8]

The *Encyclopaedia Judaica's* article under the heading *Word*
summarizes this history, praising Philo's multi-faceted thought
on the *Logos*, which draws in not only the influence of
Heraclitus, the Stoics, and Plato, but also biblical ideas of
divine creativity and immanence and the power of God's name.
The article characterizes the *Logos* of John's Gospel as a nar-
rower, partisan term and claims that John's use of it constitutes
a major rift between Jewish and Christian thought. The article
could be read as a commentary on Cairns' poem "In Lieu of
Logos":

The multi-faceted character of the Logos is reflected in the
many metaphorical epithets applied to it by Philo: "divine
thought," "the image of God," "the firstborn son," "the
archpriest," "the paraclete of humanity." Philo paved the

way for later Christian theology. In the prologue to John's Gospel (1:14) this is carried farther, and "the Word made flesh" is identified with Jesus. Philo's Logos is no more than an "archangel of many names," the rational principle in the divine nature, the creative mediator between God—the One who is all-perfect and all-good—and the world of matter, which is inherently evil; but the Johannine Logos is a separate divine entity. At this stage the Word created an impossible gulf between Judaism and its daughter faith.[9]

Sorting out the influence, salutary or pernicious, of these strains of thought would take a team of specialist historians, theologians, and linguists. If one were so inclined, one could recall and revisit the great theological controversies of the early church, some of which, such as the Monarchian controversy of the second century, dealt directly with the church's thinking and teaching about the *Logos*.[10] Also, the third-century resolutions of the church on the meaning of *Logos* may be seen directly in the creeds.

When Cairns writes about the *Logos* and its "fussy Greek ontology of diminishing returns," he may be referring to these controversies of the early Christian centuries. He might also have in mind the sort of exercise in which living faith is treated as fodder for academic disputes. In other words, it might be heretical, gnostic-tinged thought that Cairns opposes, or it might be theological controversy itself, with its tendency toward polemic that sometimes flares up to draw attention to itself, pulling attention away from ethical action in the world.

Judaic versus Christian Thought

Some analysts of religious thought see a more general and fundamental split between Jewish and Christian thinking arising here. While Western Christianity developed systems of thought and doctrine, Judaism moved in another, earthbound direction. In an essay for a volume on Jewish–Christian dialogue, the Jewish scholar Pinchas Lapide gives support to Cairns's view that thought-infused *Logos* is a foreign concept that, imported from Athens to Jerusalem, introduced theological systems of thought into the earthbound traditions of Judaism:

> The church, from its very beginnings, has been interested
> in those principal questions regarding faith, transcendental
> ideology, and the truths of salvation which are customarily
> incorporated into theological systems. The Jews, on the
> other hand, have very little theology in the Christian sense
> of this Greek word. Instead, their faith is grounded in a
> revealed way of life that makes daily deeds of faith, rather
> than faith itself, the true test of divine approval.[11]

Historians, philosophers, and theologians are trained and equipped to breathe in the atmosphere of historical ideas, but for poets the atmosphere of ideas alone must seem foreign and sterile. A literary artist—even one such as Cairns, who ponders theology—has little material to work with in a highly intellectualized Christianity.

Cairns tempers and corrects an intellectualized Christianity with the grounded quality of Hebraic thought. For the sake of his art, and perhaps for the sake of the faith itself, he identifies superfluous, philosophical speculations so that they might be pruned, and hoes around the main roots of Christianity, planted deep in the soil of ancient Israel, so that new, unpredictable creations might grow from them. He also demonstrates his affinity for Hebraic thought by his choice of scripture: Cairns acknowledges that all the scripture passages he cites in *Recovered Body* are taken from *TANAKH*, which is the translation of the Hebrew scripture preferred within English-speaking Judaism.[12]

There are significant conclusions to be drawn here. A preference for a Hebraic reading of scripture may indicate an earth-loving, creative method. A biblical approach to life may inform an artistic principle. Cairns rejects metaphysical flights of thought that would transport writers, and readers, to a destination not of this world. Cairns is at home with our decaying earth, rather than with vanishing reason.[13]

This artistic principle may also inform a theological or faith principle: out of the substance of the earth, God's word and spirit bring life into being, while the decaying earth provides a welcoming bed to which dying life returns.[14] Affirming these truths, Cairns writes as a poet of the ordinary earth, and therefore as a poet of death.

Coincidentally or not, this earthy vision sounds remarkably similar to an approach to writing poems advocated by contemporary, secular poets such as Robert Pinsky. In championing poetry that shares the virtues of prose—clear, literary earthtones, natural meanings and emotional sensibilities that fit actual human life—Pinsky has registered his mistrust of poets who never include terms of everyday "surfaces of life," from the supermarket or the garden, for example, in their work:

> . . . poets have been known, historically, to strangle their work on gobbets of poetic diction; when poetry gets too far from prose, it may be in danger of choking itself on a thick, rich handful of words. . . . What must be pointed out is the horrible ease with which a stylish rhetoric can lead poetry unconsciously to abandon life itself.[15]

Life itself is a gift of God from the good earth. Reading Cairns we are persuaded that some poets may imitate the God of Israel and follow Jesus of Nazareth, imagining life and creating visions out of soil and language.

The Body's Bawdy Tastes

Cairns has created another embodiment of his grounded Christian faith in "Loves: Magdalen's Epistle." In this poem we hear the music of faith through the imagined voice of Mary Magdalene, whom all four Gospels name first in their lists of Jesus' female disciples. In her role as a primary disciple she served Jesus faithfully in life, attended to his body in death, and greeted him beyond the grave.[16]

The poem begins not with the taste of ice cream served on a city street, as in "Necropolitan," but with the taste of bread and wine broken and poured for friends. The tongue senses a "bright, intoxicating sweetness," like love itself:

> the mystery of spirit graved
> in what is commonplace and plain—
> the broken, brittle crust, the cup.

Then the "voice" of Mary Magdalene tells of her several meetings with Jesus, including the meeting

... in the garden when,
having died and risen, he spoke
as to a maid and asked me why

I wept. When, at *any* meeting
with the Christ, was I not weeping?

A comment on this rhetorical question provides a definition of the inspiration that comes in an encounter of love:

For what? I only speculate

—brief inability to speak,
a weak and giddy troubling near
the throat, a wash of gratitude.

The description is reminiscent of Robert Frost's sequence of the creation of a poem:

A poem begins as a lump in the throat, a sense of wrong, a homesickness, a lovesickness ... it finds the thought and the thought finds the words.[17]

A lump in the throat, just beyond the taste buds of the tongue: this is the place where human love might begin as well. The order of literary creation imitates the order of incarnate love. Following Frost, we might expect that the creative process could begin with a pre-verbal twitch, a fragment of thought, a feeling of offense, or smoldering anger. Then this bit of a poem might become a thought, or a verbal texture. Through revision and craft this bit might combine with other small units of thought or sound. Then in steps of combination and rearrangement, a proto-poem might develop into a new creation of words—a poem on the page. The poem might then move again on the lips, as well as in the minds and hearts, of readers, as sound, metaphor, and meaning; and thereby do its recreating work on the perceptions of the reader, speaker, and listener.

Frost's order of artistic creation—a lump in the throat, thought, words—could be an order of life as well, an ethic, even a Christian ethic, and a rule by which people might live. For

Cairns, as a Christian, this order of art is the order of love, and therefore the order of life.

Mary Magdalene's love for Christ begins with a lump in the throat and then follows the same progression as art and love. Her tears lead to thoughtful reflection on her own life, followed by obedience in re-ordering her life and her words in response to her love:

> I think that *this* is what I'm called
> to say, this mild exhortation
>
> that one should still abide *all* love's
> embarrassments, and so resist
> the new temptation—

Cairns implies that as a poem can be brought to life through the revisions of love, so a human being can be recreated, born again, through the spiritually revising work of love: "If anyone is in Christ, there is a new creation: everything old has passed away. . . ."[18] This creative theory tracks a Christian sacramental belief about the nature of human life and of God's grace. We receive the grace of God through our senses. The psalmist wrote, "Taste and see that the Lord is good."[19]

"The new temptation" that Mary Magdalene would warn against is nothing but Cairns's thought-demon, gnosticism: religious thought divorced from the body and therefore from love.

> I have received some little bit
>
> about the glib divisions which
> so lately have occurred to you
> as right, as necessary, fit—
>
> That the body is something less
> than honorable, say, in its
> . . . appetites? That the spirit is
>
> something pure, and—if all goes well—
> potentially unencumbered
> by the body's bawdy tastes.

The problem, says Magdalene, is that this bodiless, world-denying, bifurcated spirituality results in piety without compassion, unengaged with the world. In striving for spiritual salvation the imperative to serve and to attend to other people gets lost:

This disposition, then, has led
to a banal and pious lack
of charity, and, worse, has led

more than a few to attempt some
soul-preserving severance—harsh
mortifications, manglings, all

manner of ritual excision
lately undertaken to prevent
the body's claim upon the *heart* . . .

Then the hand that trumps the strong pair of Plato and Aristotle is played, with Magdalene's insistence on the sensous requirement of love:

I fear that you presume—dissecting
the person unto something less
complex. I think you forget

you are not Greek. I think that you
forget the very issue which
induced the Christ to take on flesh.

All loves are bodily, require
that the lips part, and press their trace
of secrecy upon the one

beloved—

Again, put positively this time:

. . . Jesus, whose image I work
daily to retain. I have kissed
his feet. I have looked long

into the trouble of his face,
and met, in that intersection,
the sacred place—where body

and spirit both abide, both yield,
in mutual obsession. Yes,
if you'll recall your Hebrew *word*.

just long enough to glimpse in its
dense figure *power to produce*
you'll see as well the damage Greek

has wrought upon your tongue, stolen
from your sense of what is holy,
wholly good, fully animal—

the body which he now prepares.

In tone and substance this calls to mind the high Christology—and supreme blessing of earth—found in the first chapter of Colossians:

... for in him all the fullness of God was pleased to dwell,
and through him God was pleased to reconcile to himself
all things, whether on earth or in heaven, by making peace
through the blood of his cross.[20]

Here is an action plan: sacramental service and a program for salvation accomplished here on the earth. The things that matter to Cairns are the sacramental substances of this world, including the sensuous word, spoken, heard, and reshaped as a new creation, in and for a community.

The Creativity of the Word

The Hebrew prophets declared the unconditional creative power of God's word:

For as the rain and the snow come down from heaven, and
do not return there until they have watered the earth,
making it bring forth and sprout, giving seed to the sower

and bread to the eater,
so shall my word be that goes out from my mouth; it shall
    not return to me empty,
but it shall accomplish that which I purpose,
    and succeed in the thing for which I sent it.[21]

The word of God contains the power to create, and then to judge, promise, forgive, and renew all that the word has created. Furthermore, this power is not limited by the seasons of human life. Even at the death of the creatures of the earth, the word remains potent:

The grass withers, the flower fades,
    when the breath of the Lord blows upon it;
    surely the people are grass.
The grass withers, the flower fades;
    but the word of our God will stand forever.[22]

When a Christian poet such as Cairns works with words, he assents to this ancient understanding. He might also intuitively grasp an old, old energy in language, an energy that originates from an even earlier time than the Hebrew sources.

The Language of Myth

The structural framework on which Cairns hangs the problem of language—a dichotomy between Hebrew integration-of-life-and-law and Greek intellectual-and-spiritual-detachment—furnishes a useful analytical tool, but the matter could also be stated in a way that is fairer to the *Logos*. One might be able to unpack from *Logos*, as well as from *davar*, a set of valuable meanings. For example, Gerhard von Rad places ancient Israel's perception of the powerful word in a general context of mythical thought in which no distinction was made between the spiritual and the material, between the ideal and the real, between the word and the object: "In a way which defies precise rational clarification, every word contains something of the object itself."[23]

Historians of religion and philosophers have pointed out this unified power of language in mythical societies. Ernst Cassirer, a philosopher of culture and language, wrote:

> In its first beginnings the word still belongs to the sphere
> of mere existence: what is apprehended in it is not a signi-
> fication but rather a substantial being and power of its
> own. It does not point to an objective content but sets
> itself in the place of this content; it becomes a power
> which intervenes in empirical events and their causal
> concatenation.[24]

The world of spirits, of magic, of curses and spells, lives throughout Christian and Jewish scripture. In this world there is no separation between sacred and profane, between the spiritual and the material, the secular and the sacred.

A belief in the special power of words is found in other ancient cultures as well. When we read von Rad's description of classical Greek, for example, we hear a conception of the word, and of language, that poets of many centuries would appreciate:

> The characteristic of classical Greek is that the word oper-
> ates as a rhythmic and musical force and at the same time
> as language, as a phonetic formation, as that which con-
> veys ideas and emotions. . . . What impression may the
> Greeks have had of their own language? They must have
> had the feeling that it was mightier than they. A Greek
> word is like a solid body that the hands can grasp.[25]

Von Rad suggests that the *power to produce* (to use Cairns's words) was not only invested in *davar*, from the Hebrew scriptures and the rabbinic tradition. The power of language was a part of a general, unreflective, human understanding of how the world and words worked.

How can the Hebrew scriptures belong in any meaningful sense to people today? Because the ancient world view is so different from our own, theologians and teachers are challenged to interpret and translate ancient thought patterns to those of us who seek to understand them. The poet's task is different. A poet is free to experiment with language and to produce with creative power (the word *poem* comes from a Greek word that means "a thing created or made") new forms carrying important meaning that discursive words fail to convey.

Louis Dupré distinguishes between religious thinking and unified mythical language in this way: as mythological thinking recedes, religious reflection takes its place. For example, when the imagination dominates life, the ritual dancer becomes a god, recreating an act of creation. Such a dancer exists in the world of magic and of myth, or, as we will see in the chapter on Mark Jarman, in the world of childhood. Dupré reminds us, however, that "when the dancer realizes that he is not the god whose nature he assumes, but only represents him, he has left the purely mythical mentality"[26] and has entered the mentality of religious ritual instead.

Dupré writes that religious concepts reflect myth and use the language of myth as they attempt to "reconcile and integrate conflicting aspects of existence." Religion may employ the language of myth for reflection in an effort to heal the inevitable divisions and fissures of human life and consciousness. To put Dupré's point in another way: religious language aims beyond itself, to speak about God.

Dupré argues that poetic language has a different goal: to "reconcile the conflicting sides of existence in one dramatic vision."[27] As a language of life, poetic language resembles the primary and unreflected words of the prophets. Such words have power to do things, create things, build things—even such things as standards of ethics, justice, and truth, not to mention things of beauty. Words serve as active partners with the poet in the formation of a poem, each one adding its own ever-evolving history to the pulsing, forward-moving creation.

The danger with religious language is that it is prone to self-division—thought against thought, distinction after distinction—ultimately choking our spiritual pathways with its thick and ponderous verbiage. As we have seen, Cairns lets *Logos* and gnosticism take the blame for this objectionable consequence. But because poetry does not primarily involve analyzing or describing ideas, it is able to draw on the integrated and mythological power known in the world of scripture.

For Cairns, most essential of all is that the "power to produce" lies in the recesses of the words he uses. He holds this belief as a statement of art and of faith, knowing that the language of poetry can still invent and reinvent itself. He uses words that are lineal descendants of ancient words, still retaining their original power through centuries of change. In the ancient world words did everything that was done. God was in the words. Jeremiah wrote that the word of the Lord actually "came" to him, saying. . . .[28] Even today, words can invent and reinvent humanity.

One poem from Cairns's collection *The Translation of Babel*[29] may serve to demonstrate how poetic language reconciles and integrates conflicting aspects of existence (to return to Dupré's apt phrase). In "Coming Forth," the conflicting aspects are life and death. The poem depicts Death as a youngster, perhaps an adolescent, erupting with inappropriate laughter in reaction to pain and dying. The main force of the poem's emotion—carried under darkly amusing and mildly grotesque details of uncontrollable laughter in the face of tragedy—seems to blend with the hope inside fragile and crumbling faith. The last lines are:

I just get this quiver started

In me every time someone I know dies and stays dead.
I tremble all over and have to hold

myself, as if some crazy thing in me
were anxious to get out. I told you

I can't remember being dead. I can't.
but this weakness in my knees, or in my throat

keeps me thinking—whatever comes next
should be a thousand worlds better than this.

Human experience is not neat and orderly. Our bodies break. Our plans crumble. The Teacher, in Ecclesiastes, wrote,

I thought the dead, who have already died, more fortunate
than the living, who are still alive; but better than both is
the one who has not yet been, and has not seen the evil
deeds that are done under the sun.[30]

As sons and daughters of the earth we are dust, and to dust we shall return.[31] We are children of the broken earth and, at the same time, heirs of a renewing spirit that comes "from the four winds and breathes life to the scattered slain."[32] Cairns would tell us that hope springs from natural events in the course of life. Faith recognizes the spirit's procreating, recreating, healing desire toward reunion. The spirit of God may be a breath of creativity, a breeze of inspiration, or a powerful force that helps to heal a fragmented and withered world.

1. Scott Cairns, *Recovered Body* (New York: George Brazilier, Inc., 1998), 15.

2. Abraham J. Heschel, "Death as Homecoming,"" in *Jewish Reflections on Death*, Jack Reimer, ed. (New York: Schocken Books, 1974), 59.

3. Bengt Hagglund, *History of Theology* (St. Louis: Concordia Publishing House, 1968), 33f.

4. Hagglund, *History*, 38.

5. Throughout this chapter I use Cairns's transliteration of the Hebrew word.

6. Cairns, *Recovered Body*, 70.

7. Rene Girard, trans. Stephen Bann and Michael Metteer, *Things Hidden Since the Foundation of the World* (Stanford: Stanford University Press, 1978), 263.

8. J. N. D. Kelly, *Early Christian Doctrines* (New York: Harper and Row, 1960), 7–8.

9. *Encylopaedia Judaica*, vol. 16 (Jerusalem: Keter Publishing House, 1971), 634–635.

10. See Henry Chadwick, *The Early Church* (New York: Penguin Books, 1967).

11. Pinchas Lapide and Ulrich Luz, *Jesus in Two Perspectives* (Minneapolis: Augsburg, 1985), 18. Underlying this observation more than in the Cairns poem (although it is there as well) is a barely hidden struggle for moral high ground. When religion is analyzed according to categories of thought versus action, thought, as the self-absorbed and idle concept, loses. In other words, most of us would choose good works over right thinking. The matter is not resolved quite so simply, however. The problem for religiously sensitive souls is, as Auden wrote, quoting Cesare Pavese: "We can all do good deeds, but very few of us can think good thoughts." See Dag Hammarskjöld, *Markings*, foreword by W. H. Auden (New York: Knopf, 1965), ix. This struggle appears in intra-Christian debates as well. Among the pairings are faith versus works, right ritual versus right living, devotion versus service, etc.

12. One would make other assumptions about Cairns if he had chosen, for example, the *New Revised Standard Version*, which some might consider to be a liberal Protestant choice; or the *Jerusalem Bible*, a poetic Catholic paraphrase. Novelist Larry Woiwode makes an issue of his choice of a translation. In his book Acts, he writes, "I usually quote from the New American Standard Bible, which I find the most accurate version, verse by verse, in English, but I also refer to the King James, the

Authorized Version and the New Revised Standard Version, and a text in my computer called the Modern King James Version." Larry Woiwode, *Acts* (San Francisco: Harper, 1993), 17–18.

13. One might compare Cairns's poems with those of Wendell Berry. Both poets work close to the earth.

14. Cf. Genesis 2:7, Jeremiah 18:6, John 9:11.

15. Robert Pinsky, *The Situation of Poetry: Contemporary Poetry and Its Traditions* (Princeton: Princeton University Press, 1976), 163.

16. See, for example, John 20.

17. From a letter of January 1, 1916 to Louis Untermeyer.

18. 2 Corinthians 5:17.

19. Psalm 34:8.

20. Colossians 1:19–20a.

21. Isaiah 55:10–11.

22. Isaiah 40:7–8.

23. Gerhard von Rad, *Old Testament Theology*, Vol II (New York: Harper & Row, 1965), 81.

24. Ernst Cassirer, *The Philosophy of Symbolic Forms, Vol. 2: Mythical Thought* (New Haven: Yale University Press, 1955), 237.

25. Von Rad, 85. Here von Rad draws on a German book about the music and rhythm of classical Greek.

26. Louis Dupré, *Symbols of the Sacred* (Grand Rapids: William B. Eerdmans Publishing Company, 2001), 117.

27. Dupré, Symbols, 118.

28. Jeremiah 1.

29. Scott Cairns, *The Translation of Babel* (The University of Georgia Press, 1990).

30. Ecclesiastes 4:1–3.

31. Genesis 3:19.

32. Ezekiel 37.

Chapter 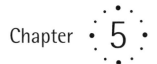 5

Death be not proud, though some have called thee
Mighty and dreadful, for thou art not so;
For those whom thou think'st thou dost overthrow
Die not, poor death; nor yet canst thou kill me.
From rest and sleep, which but thy pictures be,
Much pleasure, then from thee much more must flow;
And soonest our best men with thee do go,
Rest of their bones and soul's delivery.
Thou'rt slave to fate, chance, kings and desperate men,
And dost with poison, war, and sickness dwell;
And poppy or charms can make us sleep as well
And better than thy stroke. Why swell'st thou then?
One short sleep past, we wake eternally,
And Death shall no more; Death, thou shalt die.

John Donne (1572–1631)
Holy Sonnets: Divine Meditations

Now I lay me down to sleep,
I pray the Lord my soul to keep;
If I should die before I wake,
I pray the Lord my soul to take.

New England Primer, 1784.

. . . Our birth is but a sleep and a forgetting:
The Soul that rises with us, our life's Star,
   Hath had elsewhere its setting,
   And cometh from afar:
   Not in entire forgetfulness,
   And not in utter nakedness,
But trailing clouds of glory do we come
   From God, who is our home:
Heaven lies about us in our infancy!

Shades of the prison-house begin to close
    Upon the growing Boy,
But he beholds the light, and whence it flows
    He sees it in his joy;
The Youth, who daily farther from the east
    Must travel, still is Nature's priest. . .

William Wordsworth (1770–1850)
"Intimations of Immortality from Recollections
of Early Childhood"

Childhood and Memory:
Mark Jarman

My son, at about three-and-a-half years old, looked up at me from his tricycle one afternoon and asked with a smile, "Where is God?" He smiled again at my stammered response, but let the matter drop in favor of examining a crow's feather at the side of the road. In his first sounding of this ancient wild rose of a question, I sensed no anger, no longing, not a hint of challenge. The ground of my son's life had been prepared by the fertilizing action of the small prayers he knew, the Sunday school songs he had learned, and the bits of instruction and stray sentences of sermons he had heard. In a safe, relaxed moment, the question sprouted in the delight of a sunny afternoon. In play, he tossed out this important question. I fumbled it and tossed it back. My son seemed satisfied with this more-ritual-than-substantial interchange. Our brief exchange illustrates several attributes to guide a reading of Mark Jarman's poems of memory:

- Life experience provides the raw material of art and of faith.
- Child's play may supply a model for creating poems. An adult, recalling a childlike state of mind, engages in a spiritual exercise that may enhance faith.
- The experience of the absence of God may serve as a stage for the poetic imagination.

Where is God?

In the incident I have described, my son served as a Socratic teacher, drawing answers out of me. At that age he did not need to hear my full answer, even if I had thought of it. I might have said, "God is right here with us, in your words, in our play, in our love for one another." The slightly mischievous yet inno-cent smile on my son's face when he asked the question—Where is God?—could have been a judgment on grown-up reli-gion and church ritual. The importance of the event—for me, not for him—caused it to be impressed into my memory.

A poet might create a poem out of such a memory. Indeed, in one of Jarman's poems, a parent and a child reverse roles. The son becomes the parent. The parent becomes the child. "The Past From the Air"[1] contains this scene:

> My mother sitting next to me looks on,
> Arms folded as if to heal two bitten hands.
> I point the landmarks out, the known, unknown. . .

In another poem, "Last Suppers," a child teaches a lesson in art and theology. Jarman contrasts the peaceful, dignified tableau in Leonardo da Vinci's fresco of the Last Supper against actual family meals, "With Father drunk again and Mother silent;" or in which "Dessert was the old man's fist against his eldest // And down the punching order to my friend.

As the poem continues, just before the light on the print of the Last Supper is switched off, the youngest sister in the fam-ily points to Jesus in the print and says, "That's God." The next lines are:

> . . .You had to answer
> Before the scene went dark. You had to say,
> "Yes," to her catechism. "That is God."

This little girl, standing on a chair, reveals her knowledge of art and performs a small act of what Peter Berger calls the "human propensity to order reality."[2] Though her own experi-ence of mealtime was disordered and painful, set against the staring image of an orderly Last Supper, "before the scene went dark" the little girl found an ordering principle.

Berger writes further that for this propensity to actually order reality, for it to be held in the mind as trustworthy, somehow it must be connected to an order that transcends everyday experience:

. . . at the very center of the process of becoming fully human, at the core of *humanitas,* we find an experience of trust in the order of reality . . . there is an intrinsic impulse to give cosmic scope to this order, an impulse that implies not only that human order in some way corresponds to an order that transcends it, but that this transcendent order is of such a character that [one] can trust it.

Providing this assurance, Berger writes, is in large part the task of a parent:

Every parent (or, at any rate, every parent who loves his child) takes upon himself this representation of a universe that is ultimately in order and ultimately trustworthy. This representation can be justified only within a religious (strictly speaking a supernatural) frame of reference.

Berger believes that if this ordering assurance of parental love is not present, the cosmic, that is, religious, final truth that the child comprehends will be not love but terror:

. . . not light but darkness. The nightmare of chaos, not the transitory safety of order, would be the final reality of the human situation. For in the end, we must all find ourselves in darkness, alone with the night that will swallow us up.

Readers of Jarman's poems might understand his image of the little girl pointing out "God" and hearing a reply, as a kind of liturgical call and response, "before the scene went dark."

The Inspiration of Scripture

In Jarman's poems bits of scripture and imagined lines that merely sound like they might be scripture stand with images from daily life. Readers join Jarman on the borderland between life and death: on the mountain of revelation and change (Matthew 17, Luke 9, and Mark 9), in a hospital room, in a child's bedroom. His poems are oblique conversations, reflections of changing minds and shifting perspectives. His seven-part poem "Transfiguration" meditates on life and death. In it, we read of changing color and varying intensity of light:

They were talking to him about resurrection, about law,
    about the suffering ahead.
. . . .
About how the body, broken or burned, could live again,
    remade.
. . . .
When we brought our mother to him, we said, "Lord,
    she falls down the stairs.
She cannot hold her water . . ."
. . . .
They were talking to him about heaven, how all forms
    there were luciform,
. . . .
And they were talking about the complexities of blood
and lymph,
. . . .
I want to believe that he talked back to them, his radiant
    companions,
And I want to believe he said too much was being asked
    and too much promised.
I want to believe that that was why he shone in the eyes
    of his friends. . . .[3]

The Gospel account of the transfiguration, the public read-
ing of which occurs in many churches at the turn from
Epiphany to Lent, is the poem's transportation, moving it
along. Garrett Green writes that

> . . . scripture embodies the paradigm through which
> Christians view the world in its essential relation to God,
> the images by which God in-forms the imagination.[4]

Annie Dillard once wrote that as a child she "had a head for
religious ideas":

> They were the first ideas I ever encountered. They made
> other ideas seem mean. . . . I had miles of Bible in memory:
> some perforce, but most by hap, like the words to songs.
> There was no corner of my brain where you could not find
> . . . snarls and reels of the Bible. I wrote poems in deliber-
> ate imitation of its sounds. . . .[5]

Like Dillard, Jarman has the Bible—biblical stories and biblical sounds—running through his imagination in ways that hardly follow a strict ordering of narrated events, but that satisfy similarly equipped readers with writing that imitates the sound and authority of scripture.[6]

How does the scripture story provide Mark Jarman's "Transfiguration" with a sense of the threshold of death? In the Gospel account of this event, Jesus makes opaque comments to his disciples that his death is approaching. As the disciples walk down the mountain with Jesus, he ordered them

> . . . to tell no one about what they had seen until after the Son of Man had risen from the dead. So they kept the matter to themselves, questioning what this rising from the dead could mean.[7]

In other places such as Luke 18, Jesus speaks about going to his death in the holy city of Jerusalem:

> Then he took the twelve aside and said to them, "See, we are going up to Jerusalem, and everything that is written about the Son of Man by the prophets will be accomplished. . . . After they have flogged him, they will kill him, and on the third day he will rise again." But they understood nothing about all these things; in fact, what he said was hidden from them, and they did not grasp what was said.

Though the disciples would push all thoughts of his death from their minds, Jesus continues to guide them to this threshold, holding the past and the future before them.

Past, Present, and Future

The transfiguration of Jesus joins the past and the future together in the light of a sacred conversation. Moses and Elijah arrive from the past to talk with Jesus about the future. Both their dazzling appearance and their words disclose to Jesus' disciples a new aspect of his identity, shedding light on current events and revealing the ultimate meaning of Jesus' life and death.

Similarly, the best patterns of Christian worship will create connections with our history, current life concerns and conditions, and hope for the future. We bring to our worship the mixed emotional altitudes of our lives, including our mountaintop experiences and valleys of disappointment. This template of worship, shining with the glory of heaven, may fail us in the everyday events of our lives. If we turn to poetry, we find it a medium of art, at least as Jarman uses it, suited not for recasting life in a worship mode, but for enhancing reflections on life as it is lived on the plains of ordinary experience.

Several lines from the third section of "Transfiguration" contemplate the division of our lives into past, present, and future:

And how simple it is to see the future, if you looked at it
    like the past,
And how the present belonged to the flesh and its density
    and darkness
And was hard to talk about. Before and after were easier.
They talked about light.

In the poem's imagined universe the present belongs to the density and darkness of the flesh. The future, imagined as a transposition of the past, is easy to talk about. The present, full of the earth, is thick and heavy, overspreading and outweighing words.

Playing in Church

In a kind of sacred syntax, or order of language, human history and an eschatological horizon hang together in the scriptural imagination. Slanted and oblique language—such as the language of poetry—when dared in our day, may catch a bit of light from these horizons. (Emily Dickinson wrote, "Tell the whole truth / but tell it slant.') Jarman's creativity might seem more like idle play than like a system or formula of writing. His poems exhibit a jostled playfulness as well as a repeating strain of humor.

Church ideas, church talk, church smells and sounds, must have been part of Jarman's childhood. As the child of a minister, he probably had the experience, shared by many ministers' kids, of *playing* in the church. While most church-going children come into the public spaces to attend Sunday school and a service, for the children of ministers the church building often becomes a second home. They experience the furnace room, the cleaning closet, the kitchen, the choir loft, or the sacristy, as a playground and a weekday hideout. Jarman knows that ministers' kids are among those who breathe in remnants of prayer and worship that hang in the air, along with the smell of wine, candle smoke, and soap; the sacraments and quarrels, the vigils and meetings.

The image of a child wandering or running back and forth in the aisles of a church furnishes a model both for prayer and for creative method. The child indulges in reflective play within a place built to foster concern for the needs of others, whether in the town or the whole world. Jarman shows that the verbal sanctuary of religious thought may be occupied playfully, and that irreverence is not sacrilege.

> Hands folded to construct a church and steeple,
> A roof of knuckles, outer walls of skin,
> The thumbs as doors, the fingers bent within
> To be revealed, wriggling, as "all the people,"
> All eight of them, enmeshed, caught by surprise. . . .

Wonder is an innocent outlook, belonging properly to childhood. In worship, the children of God learn wonder again.

> After the praying, after the hymn-singing,
> After the sermon's trenchant commentary
> On the world's ills, which makes ours secondary,
> After communion, after the hand-wringing,
> And after peace descends upon us, bringing
> Our eyes up to regard the sanctuary
> And how the light swords through it . . . .

Wonder, like childhood itself, largely passes away with the years. In the order of growth, adults bow under layers of sobering experiences piled on through the years:

> There is one stubborn remnant of your cares
> Intact. There is still murder in your heart.[8]

But a bit of wonder remains in adults. It may be mined through memory, in a kind of pilgrimage of return. The Christian idea of pilgrimage begins to describe the desire to return to a place of wonder. Christian pilgrims choose holy destinations such as Rome, Jerusalem, or Lourdes. The primary route for pilgrims, however, goes back to Eden. We still want to play in that garden, or our grandmother's garden, or at the lake, or on the field, as we did when we were children.

The Dutch historian Johan Huizinga writes—with reference mainly to archaic cultures—that poetry used to have social and liturgical as well as aesthetic functions, and that furthermore, to the ancients, poetry was "born in and as play." He raises up the ancient type of the *vates,* the possessed, God-smitten prophet/ poet who brought meaning and order out of sacred word play on behalf of the community. One might see Jarman as a Californian *vatic* poet, standing on the edge of self-serious institutions in the place where a prophet might stand, except that this poet/prophet is neither religiously nor ethically oriented in the way one might expect a prophet to be. He does not directly address the hypocrisies of the establishment. The artist as poet/prophet occupies a different place. Without an institutional program of reform and without malice, the poet-with-God-on-his-mind turns and twists sacred things, rearranges and bends theological concepts, swirling the shapes and shards of church trappings.

Poetry as Play

In the United States of America some young men are paid millions of dollars a year to play children's games such as basketball or baseball, while the rest of us spend our leisure time watching them play. Team owners, advertisers, and merchants can make large and small amounts of money from this arrangement. Play and economics—children's games and financial ambition— intersect in the big business and entertainment culture of American professional sports. We follow professional sports teams for a host of reasons. Among these are pride of place, a need for competition that can be satisfied safely by cheering, tribal bonding, and the continuing enjoyment of childhood memories of heroes and of recalled dreams of achievement. We watch those who play well because youth (even fading youth), competition, and excellent execution of athletic movements are among the basic victories of the human race.

Like the athlete's sport, the poet's craft is a kind of play, despite the absence of the athlete's economic rewards. As the most accomplished athletes have turned their talents into achievement through years of discipline and training, the poet has spent years studying and reading, writing and revising, probably not in preparation for writing poetry, but out of inclination toward and interest in the subject. The poet develops a creative talent that takes raw material, drawn from history, observation, and experience, and shapes it into art.

In his book *The Magic of Ritual*, Tom Driver writes about ritual in words that could apply to a reading of Jarman's poems:

> In Christian theological perspective, work done playfully is a sign of grace. That is, it cannot be accounted for rationally, for it is transformative work accomplished through play.[9]

Driver wants to distinguish ritual from *art*, as we know it in complex societies. Ritual, he writes, is "work done playfully" while art is "play done workfully." Underlying this rather awkward thought is the belief that art is constrained by society's conventions, or, one might assume, by literary conventions such as poetic forms.

For Driver, however, ritual action is unconstrained and unplanned and, at the same time, is useful to a community both socially and recreationally. He makes a further observation that people engaged in ritual are "almost always conscious of the absurdity, the contradiction lying with ritual pretension." In other words, transforming ritual is carried out with half-a-smile. Even though Driver does not seem to have poetry in mind here, his thoughts provide helpful insight into Jarman's poems in three ways:

First, Jarman's poems build on given traditions of form and content, and therefore are a given cultural work—that is, they are not merely the record of imaginative glides of the poet's mind.

Second, his poems often give the impression of being created in a mental process resembling play. Sometimes the content also has a playful quality. Americans, obsessed with being at play—especially in expensive outdoor activities as a reward for success—might discover that in reading some contemporary poetry they are participating with the poet in recreational, literary play.

Third, Jarman's poems give a hint of not taking themselves too seriously as cultural creations. This poetic self-effacement strikes the reader as humility (one of the classic Christian virtues). Continuing in a Christian perspective, the humor that underlies many of Jarman's works might also be seen as a sign of grace.

The Inspiration of Childhood

Jarman knows the history and fundamentals of his field. He advocates formal poetry that uses the "meters of the English tradition," in the "verse forms associated with those meters,"[10] but the substance of his poems is often his own memory and reflection. Through heart-play and word-play he sifts the sand of his own days to disclose its outstanding emotional moments. He sets out this biographical method in a reflective line in the body of his poem "Ground Swell":

You write about the life that's vividest.
And if that is your own, that is your subject.

To reflect upon one's childhood is to recall a time when life showed its brightest colors. Childhood is the time of uninhibited movement and unencumbered grace. In childhood, formative stories take root, language soaks in, and faith puts down its tap root. As described in Genesis, Eden was the early childhood of the human race, the innocent time, the time of walking with God in the garden, the time without death or even the knowledge of death.

Other qualities of the heart, vices as well as virtues, are first formed in the early years of life as well. In an essay, with reference to Ezra Pound, Jarman wrote: "Prejudice begins in childhood."[11] As ideas planted in the new soil of childhood tend to last into adulthood, the grown man hides the child he used to be within his adult body. That "child" retains childlike perceptions and emotions, even though they are often overlaid with more mature views.

Throughout his life a man is his father's son, yet in peculiar moments he may recognize his father in himself. When a man's first child is born, the child becomes a father, and once this milestone has occurred, his perceptions of his own father are forever altered.

In one of Jarman's poems, a father, saddened by a small failure, steals away for a moment to the memory of his childhood and to the hope for the future carried in his own child's life:

> To lie in your child's bed when she is gone
> Is calming as anything I know. To fall
> Asleep, her books arranged above your head,
> Is to admit that you have never been
> So tired, so enchanted by the spell
> Of your grown body.[12]

Childhood is a remembered place and an imagined dreamland that inspires Jarman's poems. He knows, of course, that Eden does not last. The child must grow into a man, and that man must die. The pole points on the axis of existence are named Eden and apocalypse, childhood and death, life renewed and life ended. The Christian faith produces its music for the heart by playing on strings held in tension between these two poles.

Crossing Over and Back

A child "sails" through the years (including the stormy sea of adolescence) into adulthood. While a person leaves childhood forever, the geography, lessons, and feelings from those years may be recalled and revisited. The years chart a pilgrimage, recording forward motion toward new insights and backward movement for the sake of remembering the best experiences and appropriating valuable lessons.

Death as a voyage to the unknown is a common trope of Christian and pagan lore. The last of Jarman's "Unholy Sonnets"[13] employs this theme in a religiously empathetic death poem. It is a composition of cosmic scope:

> If God survives us, will his kingdom come?
> But let's row out to sea and ship the oars

And watch the planet drown in meteors.
If God forgives us, surely he will come.
Can we nail up a man and do the same
To a child? Yes. And drive the spikes through tears.
But let's row out to sea and watch the stars.
No matter what we do, they are the same,
Crossing the bleeding sky on shining feet,
Walking on water toward us, and then sinking.
Surely when he grew up, God must have known
What sort of death was waiting for one thinking
That with his coming history was complete.
We'll greet him as the children would have done.

The image of death as a voyage on a river to a boundless sea reminds the reader of Tennyson's "Crossing the Bar." Jarman's poem continues with reference to the sea above us: the night sky with its display of stars. Humbled in life and death by the majesty of this vista, we encounter children engaging in sacrament-like exchanges with God. The stage of the ocean under the night sky reflects beams of light: God is like us, we are like God; God has greeted us, we will greet God. Under the unchanging panoply of the stars, we change places and identities in the sacrifice of prayer: God becomes us; we become God. Within the fellowship of this mysterious exchange we sense a Christian order of life.

Writers such as Charles Williams and C. S. Lewis[14] have portrayed the sacramental borderland between heaven and earth. They have depicted a permeable boundary that the spirit and the body may cross, joining one another and then separating again. They tell tales of the unity of body and spirit, of earth and heaven, of human and divine, building upon similar biblical stories narrated of Eden, Bethlehem, or of the Holy City in the book of Revelation.

Truly I tell you, unless you change and become like
children, you will never enter the kingdom of heaven.

Unholy Sonnets

The music of Jarman's "Unholy Sonnets" may be heard as counterpoint to John Donne's "Holy Sonnets." What makes

Jarman's sonnets unholy? One might venture to say that Jarman names his poems unholy, not because they are blasphemous or heretical but because they are not set apart (the meaning of holy) by history and by a scripture-limned piety such as Donne's. Jarman's poems are constructed not so much from learned sacred history as out of ordinary life events, washed in the syntax of scripture. Donne meditated on scripture. Jarman imaginatively recreates experience and thought. Some of his poems toss theological terms and religious thoughts together with his own memories and experiences.

One could argue, however, that the two sets of sonnets— their composition separated by four hundred years—are not as different as a reader might expect. Both poets draw on images of childhood. Denis Donoghue writes how, in a sermon of 1619, John Donne preached on the text from Ecclesiastes 12:

> Remember your creator in the days of your youth, before
> the days of trouble come, and the years draw near when
> you will say, 'I have no pleasure in them.'

Donne stressed the word *remember*, since, writes Donoghue, "memory, understanding and will form the great medieval triad, the faculties of the soul."[17] Donne's poem "Good Friday, 1613, Riding Westward" includes these lines:

> Though these things, as I ride, be from mine eye,
> They are present yet unto my memory.
> For that looks towards them; and Thou look'st towards me,
> O Saviour, as Thou hang'st upon the tree.

Donoghue points out how Donne explores his images in a theater of memory. His comment, written about Donne, could nearly fit Jarman as well:

> He is a geographer of passion, moving from one world to
> another: planets, star, the sun, meteors, compass, map, and
> so forth.[18]

God with Us

Jarman's method of treating theological material might be called inductive. Peter Berger defines inductive faith as

> ... a religious process of thought that begins with facts of human experience ... inductive faith moves from human experience to statements about God, deductive faith from statements about God to interpretations of human experience.[19]

The first of Jarman's "Unholy Sonnets" begins as an address to God in a traditionally pious manner. Then he continues with an outpouring of imaginative titles for the divine. Though the poetic form is strict, the theological play is light and irreverent, like a juggler's sleight of hand. The play around God's names echoes biblical and liturgical use, drawing in not only childlike concerns but also terms from science, technology, and more:

> Dear God, Our Heavenly Father, Gracious Lord,
> Mother Love and Maker, Light Divine,
> Atomic Fingertip, Cosmic Design,
> First Letter of the Alphabet, Last Word,
> Mutual Satisfaction, Cash Award,
> Auditor Who Approves our Bottom Line,
> Examiner Who Says That We Are Fine,
> Oasis That All Sands Are Running Toward.
>
> I can say almost anything about you,
> O Big Idea, and with each epithet,
> Create new reasons to believe or doubt you ....

Doxological, philosophical, and spiritual thoughts try to reach beyond the limits of human sensory experience. God is the highest thought, the extreme example. To some ears the poem sounds like a parody of medieval scholastic theology. One might recall St. Anselm's ontological proof for the existence of God.[20] Anselm wrote, "beyond doubt, something than which nothing greater can be thought exists in the intellect as well as in reality. And this art Thou, our Lord."[21]

Medieval scholastic theology constructed complex and rational speculative systems of thought. Jarman's poem plays off this material as it catalogues the best-we-can-hope-for in a list of the possibilities drawn from life-as-we-know-it:

> Black Hole, White Hole, Presidential Jet.
> But what's the anything I must leave out? You
> Solve nothing but the problems that I set.

One of the "problems set" by the postulate of God is the problem of suffering and the inevitable end of human life. Ideas, big ideas, good or even brilliant ideas, do not satisfy at the moments of final importance. We need God, or a reasonable facsimile, closer at hand. In the seventeenth "Unholy Sonnet" we read of the informal qualities of God's immanence:

> God like a kiss, God like a welcoming,
> God like a hand guiding another hand
> And raising it or making it descend,
> God like the pulse point and its silent drumming,
> And the tongue going to it, God like the humming
> Of pleasure if the skin felt it as sound . . . .

God is easily discovered in these transparent spiritual moments, but what about in the darker times of life, the tedium, the painful parts? After satisfying times of communion in the warmth of a familiar congregation, even after solo theological climbs up steep cliffs of paradox where hope is a handhold, the bedrock fact of non-existence awaits below. The dead are no longer welcomed and no longer welcome in the communities of the living.

God Hidden

The next line strikes an important theme in Jarman's poetic conception of God:

> God like the hidden wanting to be found

The proposition that God could be hidden from the world, from human senses, from thought and even from the imagination, emerges as a possibility in Jarman's poems. Karl Barth wrote that

> God does not belong to the objects which we can always subjugate to the process of our viewing, conceiving and expressing and therefore our spiritual oversight and control. In contrast to that of all other objects, God's nature is not one which in this sense lies in the sphere of our power. God is inapprehensible.[22]

God seems absent. God is hidden. These assertions, arising from deep within the heart of the religion of Israel, and confessed by the church, provide a point at which human freedom and God's revelation may meet.

Dietrich Bonhoeffer, developing Luther's thought on the hiddenness of God, writes that "God lets us live in the world without the working hypothesis of God."[23] Human freedom is an unqualified gift. A human being is like an adolescent set free to live in the world as if the parent were not around. We live our years in the kind of freedom a child experiences when her parents drop her off at the carnival gate. With a mixture of exhilaration and fear we sense this freedom as an adventure.

For Barth, human acknowledgment of God's hiddenness is the ground of God's revelation to humanity and therefore the ground of faith, by which human beings receive God's revelation:

> The confession of God's hiddenness is the confession of God's revelation as the beginning of our cognizance of God . . . the emphasis in the confession of God's hiddenness is . . . first and decisively that of gratitude.[24]

Throughout Jarman's poems God's absences are noted with wonder, as in this passage from the fourth of his "Unholy Sonnets":

> Amazing to believe that nothingness
> Surrounds us with delight and lets us be,
> And that the meekness of nonentity,
> Despite the friction of the world of sense,
> Despite the leveling of violence,

Is all that matters. All the energy
We force into the matchhead and the city
Explodes inside a loving emptiness.

Still, human beings need assurance of transcendence. In every stage of life and in all circumstances people continue to ask, "Where is God?"

The question arises in the mourning that follows tragedy and loss. Persecuted and oppressed people have voiced the question not as a rhetorical rose of thought but as a thorn in their suffering. Unbelievers have issued this question as a challenge to those whose faith is sustained—in the only way faith can be sustained—against appearance, proof, and circumstances.

Being blind, faith bumps and crashes and is frequently wounded, sometimes mortally. However, faith finds encouragement occasionally: a word of direction, a helpful handhold, a sign of spring, or a word of forgiveness. Children have eyes for finding these assurances of faith and ears for hearing them. They notice them in the grace of their innocence and detect them through the suppleness of their imaginations. Children often can find stand-ins for God that speak God's word and signify God's presence.

The Worry Bird

Throughout Jarman's poems, in the absence of God, little idols occupy the void along with idle questions and bits broken off from the material of the world. All these reside in the poet's memory under the scrawled heading of GOD. The poem "The Worry Bird" begins,

God was an idea before he was an image.

The next lines lead us into a life memory:

And yet there are things like the worry bird
That stay with us through life and intercede
With an old darkness, filling an old need.

That "God was an idea before he was an image" is a sly admission, risking interpretation as an atheistic creed of God as merely a creation of human thought, a projection to satisfy human need. The line could be read as well, following Genesis and John's Gospel, in the order of a *Logos* theology: God, beginning in a word and in words, becoming incarnate, imagined, in creation and in human flesh. A child's companion—a teddy bear or, to Jarman, a "worry bird"—serves as a focal point for concerns, and as a source of comfort.

In Sonnet 15 of "Unholy Sonnets," a bird appears again. Jarman writes:

> A useful God will roost in a bird-box,
> Wedge-head thrust out, red-feathered in the sun. . . .

Returning to "The Worry Bird," life continues, and stuffed animals are put away,

> The worry bird takes on another form
> And watches with another shade of interest,
> Circling among the other distant images
> That used to help and still do. Mirages
> Of comfort, they can bring a kind of rest
> Anyone who has been a child can know.

The theologian Jurgen Moltmann points toward a universal meaning of a bird in relation to death:

> We are familiar with very old religious ideas expressed in
> the pictures of early peoples, where the immortal soul of a
> human being is shown departing from the body after
> death, leaving that body behind as a lifeless corpse, while
> the soul returns to its eternal home in heaven beyond
> earth. The ancient Egyptians imagined the soul as a bird,
> with the human face of the dead person, and Elisabeth
> Kübler-Ross found a striking number of butterflies in
> the pictures painted by children in Auschwitz.[25]

A bird may also serve as an image of God, or of God's messenger: a thrilling, wild creature who can ride the wind yet still descend as a provider and caretaker:

... in a howling wilderness waste;
he shielded him, cared for him,
guarded him as the apple of his eye.
As an eagle stirs up its nest, and hovers over its young;
as it spreads its wings, takes them up,
and bears them aloft on its pinions. . . .[26]

The bird of prey dives to capture and to wound.[27] Clifford Green writes that God "captures" people through their imaginations, in "the only kind of conquest that leaves them free."[28]

In the Gospels, another bird—this time a dove—descends on Jesus of Nazareth as he stands in the river of time, on the border of the promised land, to "convict" and "capture" him with the Spirit of God. Each of the Gospels describes the Holy Spirit descending on Jesus in the form of a dove, the image of the Spirit circling and hovering over the geography and history of earth.[29] The poet and the child, the child in the poet, might be the first to notice.

---

1. Mark Jarman, *Questions for Ecclesiastes* (Ashland, Oregon: Storyline Press, 1998), 76.

2. Peter L. Berger, *A Rumor of Angels: Modern Society and the Rediscovery of the Supernatural* (Garden City: Anchor Books, 1970), 55–58. The three passages quoted are also found here.

3. Jarman, *Questions for Ecclesiastes*, 17–21.

4. Garrett Green, *Imagining God: Theology and the Religious Imagination* (San Francisco: Harper and Row, 1989), 108.

5. Annie Dillard et al., *Incarnation: Contemporary Writers on the New Testament*, ed. Alfred Corn (New York: Penguin Books, 1990), 27–28.

6. Poets might help students of the Bible find new ways of hearing a text. For example, one could listen to English words—or Greek or Hebrew words—simply for their aural qualities, apart from their meaning. An offbeat exercise like this could serve as an occasional corrective—and relief—from the historical/critical/theological method that asks students to pile up textual analysis and historical reconstruction (what a text meant to other people) and, from that data, to dust off a few specks of contemporary application. For copious examples of this, see any volume of *The Interpreter's Bible* (Nashville: Abingdon Press).

7. Mark 9:9–10.

8. Jarman, *Questions for Eccclesiastes*, 52, 64.

9. Tom Driver, *The Magic of Ritual* (San Francisco: Harper, 1991), 99.

10. See Jarman's book on contemporary poets who write in traditional forms: *Rebel Angels: 25 Poets of the New Formalism*, edited by Mark Jarman and David Mason (Ashland, Oregon: Storyline Press, 1998).

11. Mark Jarman, *The Secret of Poetry* (Ashland, Oregon: Storyline Press, 2001), 61.

12. Jarman, *Questions for Ecclesiastes*, 31.

13. Jarman, *Questions for Ecclesiastes*, 51–70.

14. See C. S. Lewis's essay, "The Novels of Charles Williams" in *C.S. Lewis on Stories and other essays*, ed. Walter Hooper (New York: Harcourt, Brace Jovanovich, 1982), 21–27.

15. Matthew 18:3.

16. A careful study might even conclude that Jarman's poems are the more traditionally pious.

17. In *Atlantic Brief Lives: A Biographical Companion to the Arts*, ed. Louis Kronenberger and Emily Beck (Boston: Little, Brown and Co., 1965), 232–234.

18. *Atlantic Brief Lives*, 232–234.

19. Berger, *A Rumor of Angels*, 57.

20. St. Anselm of Canterbury's (1033–1109) "proof" for the existence of God comes from the nature of existence itself, especially as projected in human thought. Anselm wrote, "To put it simply, we can imagine a perfect being, and so a perfect being, namely God, must exist."

21. Paul Tillich, *A History of Christian Thought* (New York: Harper and Row, 1968), 158f.

22. Karl Barth, *Church Dogmatics, Vol. II: The Doctrine of God* (Edinburgh: T & T Clark, 1957), 187.

23. Green, 147. Green quotes Bonhoeffer's *Letters from Prison*.

24. Barth, 192.

25. Leroy S. Rouner, ed., *If I Should Die* (South Bend: University of Notre Dame Press, 2001), 54.

26. Deuteronomy 32:10–11.

27. Recall Geoffrey Hill's image of a bird of prey in his poem "Genesis."

28. Green, *Imagining God*, 147.

29. Matthew 3, Mark 1, Luke 3, John 1.

Chapter 6

There is no speech, nor are there words;
their voice is not heard;
yet their voice goes out through all the earth,
and their words to the end of the world.

Psalm 19

Under the shadow of your throne
Your saints have dwelt secure.

Isaac Watts (1674–1748)
"O God, our help in ages past"

God can only be present in creation under
the form of absence. . . . To love truth
means to endure the void and, as a result,
to accept death.

Simone Weil (1909–1945)
Gravity and Grace

∴6∴
Kneeling in the Dark: R. S. Thomas

In these lines from his 1968 poem "Kneeling,"[1] readers of R. S. Thomas's poems will recognize a posture often found in his poetry:

> Moments of great calm,
> Kneeling before an altar
> Of wood in a stone church
> In summer, waiting for the God
> To speak; the air a staircase
> For silence; the sun's light
> Ringing me, as though I acted
> A great role. And the audiences
> Still; all that close throng
> Of spirits waiting, as I,
> For the message.

Terms typical of Thomas's poems are introduced here: kneeling, wood, church, waiting, silence. A more complete title for this chapter might be "Kneeling Silently by a Tree in the Dark," the four main terms of which provide a frame for the thoughts about death and darkness in the works of this Welsh poet.

Thomas's religious vision frequently has been described as bleak or dour.[2] In addition, Donald Davie's assessment of Thomas's poems as "graceless" cannot be entirely discounted.[3] However, a more accurate appraisal of Thomas might view his poetically invoked silence and darkness, indeed the absence of God, as the field and frame of traditional Christian spirituality. In other words, the absence of sound and of light that Thomas imagines are the very absences that Judaism and Christianity have known as sanctuaries, preludes, and even signs, of God's presence. Aspects and images of absence frequently shift and overlap in Thomas's poems.

Kneeling

The quieting first line of "Kneeling" suggests a summer devotional poem, even a vacation or a pilgrimage poem. The next two lines illustrate a privileged position, that of a penitent or a communicant kneeling before an altar made of wood. There is a sense of weary, heroic healing here, a practiced resignation in a posture of humble waiting. The psalmist wrote,

> Wait for the Lord;
> be strong, and let your heart take courage;
> wait for the Lord.[4]

While the vision here is a comfortable one, with the darkness set against a nimbus of light, in many of Thomas's other poems there is no such relief from the menacing dark. In the roughness of Thomas's lines, in their persistent theological questioning that sounds like crying in the dark, these poems create a general atmosphere of uncomfortable night.

The apostle Paul wrote that the whole creation waits for promised redemption:

> We know that the whole creation has been groaning in labor pains until now; and not only the creation, but we ourselves, who have the first fruits of the Spirit, groan inwardly while we wait for adoption, the redemption of our bodies.[5]

Some who wait may tap their feet impatiently. Others may fold their hands, bow their heads, and kneel in silent prayer. In Thomas's poems, one imagines waiting as a kind of spiritual listening.

Waiting is a word that may refer to service,[6] as in waiting on tables. For Christians, service denotes ministry. Ministry, in its turn, describes a major thrust of Christian communal and individual life. The posture of kneeling as one waits might be read as evidence of devotion: a life turned to God and to others in service. If there is a rest implied in this image of waiting, it might be the rest given as a peace of purpose in God's kingdom.

Waiting does not always conclude peacefully, however. In a poem entitled "Waiting for It,"[7] published nearly ten years after "Kneeling," Thomas imagines a less placid scene at waiting's end:

> in the small hours
> of belief the one eloquence
>
> to master is that
> of the bowed head, the bent
> knee, waiting, as at the end
>
> of a hard winter
> for one flower to open
> on the mind's tree of thorns.

William Davis has called Thomas a poet in an apocalyptic mode,[8] a poet of the end times, of the end of society, of the end of history, and of our collective consciousness. In the Bible, Genesis is the *alpha*, the beginning. The book of Revelation is the *omega*, the end. Another name for Revelation is *Apocalypse*, from the Greek word for revelation. Cultural commentators called the last half of the twentieth century an apocalyptic age, because of the looming threat of nuclear destruction; the first years of the twenty-first century are even less settled. Those of any time who want to read signs of the end in current events will find such signs.

Davis notes further that Thomas's way of wading into the apocalyptic night is "traditionally mystical" and therefore allows "a ray of hope at the end." Perhaps it would be more accurate in Thomas's case not to identify a ray of light at the end, but to say that the darkness itself seems alive with potential. However, to say that a poet is traditionally mystical is to say that he stands within a deep stream of theological interpretation, reaching back past Nicaea, which honors Christian teaching with ritual and service rather than honoring Christian doctrine with theology. In other words, the mysticism to which Davis refers is none other than the tradition of the Church that has developed through various activities of ministry, including contemplative modes of prayer, meditation guided by scripture, devotional study, and reflection inspired by corporate worship.

However one may choose to read the poem "Waiting for It"—as waiting for the end of one's life, or for the end of the world, or for the end of something else—one should note the posture in the poem: a bowed head and bent knee.

Oliver Clément, an authority on Christian mysticism, claims that Christianity knows nothing of the oriental technique of postures and that there is nothing mechanical or magical about any body position.[9] However, following Origen, he insists on the following postures for Christian worship:

> . . . for praise, worship and thanksgiving, pray standing
> up with out-stretched hands; for penitence or intercession,
> pray kneeling.

To look upon a person kneeling is to behold one who has in some sense submitted, whether in defeat or surrender. Kneeling is the posture of the prisoner and the knight, as well as of the priest and the communicant, all of whom kneel before their masters and their lords. Each must wait: one for a sentence and for the dishonor of punishment; one for a sword of battle and for honor in a kingdom on earth; one for the sword of the word and for honor in God's kingdom; one for the grace of bread and wine. Paradoxically, both judgment and the ministrations of love come to those who kneel.

Dom Gregory Dix writes that the practice of kneeling at the altar for communion began in the early Middle Ages in the Latin West.[10] The images of kneeling in Thomas's poems must owe something to this continuing eucharistic tradition in the Church of Wales, but to understand Thomas's meaning of kneeling one must cast back further than the Christian era. Thomas's kneeling figures also represent and imitate the posture of bending within aboriginal societies. For example, the poem "Forest Dwellers"[11] begins:

> Men who have hardly uncurled
> from their posture in the
> womb. Naked. Heads bowed, not
> in prayer, but in contemplation
> of the earth they came from,

that suckled them on the brown
milk that builds bone not brain.

Kneeling is an interim position. A prone position is intended and terminal, and, given the construction of our bodies, so is standing upright. Thomas wonders on behalf of humankind:

Who called them forth to walk
in the green light, their thoughts
on darkness?

When we stand, we are mobile and responsible, but, given life's circumstances, our fears often lead us to bow and bend again. In a poem entitled "Bent"[12] the poet expands the images of kneeling to include other bent postures of earth children suckled "on the brown / milk that builds bone not brain," who labor for wisdom and for insight into God's purposes:

Heads bowed
    over the entrails,
over the manuscript, the
block, over the rows
    of swedes.

Do they never look up?
    Why should one think
that to be on one's knees
    is to pray?

Thomas's earth children are meant to stand, but there is a weakness about their faces and heads that compromises their evolved dignity. In the lines that follow, "the weight of the jaw" may imply an overloaded value of words, especially of spoken words. As the weight of our words fails to invoke or even describe God, our bodies collapse again to silent devotion:

The aim is to walk tall
    In the sun.
Did the weight of the jaw
    bend their backs,

keeping their vision
 below the horizon?

Two million years
 in straightening them
  out, and they are still bent
 over the charts, the instruments,
  the drawing-board,
 the mathematical navel
  that is the wink of God.

In "Bent" the bending of the knee does not signify church devotion (and actually is not quite kneeling), but rather invokes the idea of scientific and technological research. Thomas sees in scientific research some residue of spiritual devotion and seems to allow the religious value of such activity. In fact, in these bent, brainy activities God is nearly present, winking and coaxing human beings on to more scientific exploration.

In "Children's Song,"[13] an early poem, Thomas sketches not the earthbound movements of forest dwellers but the scrambling play of children:

We live in our own world,
A world that is too small
For you to stoop and enter
Even on hands and knees. . . .

Adults want to kneel to enter the world of children, but they cannot. Elsewhere in his poems other barriers also restrict and frustrate human intentions, at least temporarily. For example, the poem "In a Country Church," considered below, depicts a pious person kneeling at an altar but receiving no illuminating presence and no word in return, seeing only a barren cross and an abandoned sanctuary heavy with silence.

Silence

Evelyn Underhill described the temple of Israel in these words:

> It was . . . the House where God . . . was believed to dwell
> undiscerned; in a way so entirely supernatural, so com-
> pletely transcending all our apprehensions and thoughts,
> that only the dark emptiness of this secret shrine could
> suggest it. For it is a mark of Israel's spiritual genius, that
> from the first the Jew placed Reality within mystery: and
> here, perhaps, is the source of his intense aversion from all
> images of the Divine.[14]

Underhill's illustration establishes a lineage for Thomas's
Christian spirituality of absence. In scripture and in the broad
stream of tradition, beginning in ancient Israel, there is presence
in a sacred absence of silence and darkness. The silent, imageless
holy of holies is not an austere, puritanical Protestant atmos-
phere. The empty place has power to draw people into the pres-
ence of God. Though Thomas's images seem dark and heavy,
they carry the darkness of quiet nights far from city lights. Being
attuned to nature, they speak to the senses, and, paradoxically,
to visual art and music. In an interview, Thomas said,

> My wife is a painter; I should have been a musician so that
> we could have designed a church and made music in it
> that would have been a little nearer the way in which God
> worships himself in mountains, flowers, and bird-song.[15]

Those who listen to their environment and to the people
around them may respond with silent thoughts. Those who have
sensed God's silent presence in the temple worship in silence:

> But the Lord is in his holy temple;
> Let all the earth keep silence before him![16]

Elijah heard God in the sound of sheer silence.[17] In our own
day, Quakers are adept at adoring the wonder of silence at an
interior altar, a shrine within the heart. Silence is the book in
which God's word is written, for faith to read.

Thomas's championing of silence in the face of other kinds
of religious devotion challenges the loud preaching tradition of
some forms of Protestantism. His poetry of devotion operates
without a net of warm feelings, without a safety cord of senti-
mental language. His poems do not even make promises of spir-

itual consummation or communion. With a starkness that could disturb a religious sensibility, Thomas neither declares nor implies that God can be found or known in this devotional silence, as, for example, traditional Protestantism teaches that God is available through means of the spoken word and the sacraments.

In some of the poems cited above, and in many others, Thomas seems to deny the traditional presence of God. One should see this priest's apparent atheism not as scandal or as denial of the faith, but as affirmation. Clément writes that

> contemporary atheism, to the extent that it is not stupidity but a purifying revolt, could be understood in a new way, as the path of "unknowing" that is not an intellectual path but is pure adoration.[18]

One path of unknowing—one negative way to God—for Thomas seems to lead through the shelter of the church to a stage outside in the natural world. He looks through the provisional furnishings of the nave to a natural temple of God. No pantheist, Thomas might be called a contextual Christian poet. He writes from and through the kneelers, the altars, churches, farms, and fields of Wales.

An interesting contrast may be seen between Thomas and Philip Larkin in their reactions to the silence of an empty church. Larkin writes, in "Church Going,"[19]

> Once I am sure there's nothing going on
> I step inside, letting the door thud shut.
> Another church: matting, seats, and stone
> And little books; sprawlings of flowers, cut
> For Sunday, brownish now; some brass and stuff
> Up at the holy end; the small, neat organ;
> And a tense, musty, unignorable silence,
> Brewed God knows how long. Hatless, I take off
> My cycle-clips in awkward reverence.

Larkin's narrator enters the sacred, silent space as a foreigner, perhaps as an awkward guest. As the poem goes on, he is not sure whether he stands there sheltered as a friend or as a timid adversary of the place that has attracted him. The silence is not crisp with anticipation; it is musty and tense with a past potency. The poet stares and observes but does not kneel. He does not engage the silence. His only spiritual movement is a gesture of civility: he removes his cycle clips. He never coils into an athlete's crouch to sense the quiet or to twitch at movements around him, as Thomas's figures often do.

Compare Thomas's poem, "In A Country Church"[20]:

> To one kneeling down no word came,
> Only the wind's song, saddening the lips
> Of the grave saints, rigid in glass;
> Or the dry whisper of unseen wings,
> Bats not angels, in the high roof.
>
> Was he balked by silence? He kneeled long,
> And saw love in a dark crown
> Of thorns blazing, and a winter tree
> Golden with fruit of a man's body.

This is lively silence. Kneeling, the poet participates in a service, a memorial, one might even say the anticipation of a sacramental meal. The significance of sanctuarial silence to Thomas is as a setting for devotional procession, not as a fortress for ecclesiastical control of souls. In the Larkin poem the church visitor notices all the ornaments and appointments and feels awkward among them. He perceives an arrangement of objects that have lost their animating vigor. In Thomas's poem an unusual congregation and choir—stained glass saints and bats on the wing—turn the devotional to a proper contemplation: the crucifix on the wall, described as a composite of nature. Simone Weil wrote:

> Religion, in so far as it is a source of consolation is a hindrance to true faith: in this sense atheism is purification. I have to be atheistic with the part of myself which is not made for God. Among those men in whom the supernatural part has not been awakened, the atheists are right and the believers wrong.[21]

Thomas's devotion sounds like an activity set strangely against more familiar piety. Through idols and innocent fabrication, he listens to the sound of nothing until he notices life in the breath of the wind, emotions in lead glass, messages on the wings of bats, and finally a promised love as a gift on the cross. Significantly, the thorns on the dark crown blaze, lighting the darkness.

Darkness

Many of Thomas's poems show little redemptive light. They lead the reader on rough paths, into ordinary but menacing darkness in which one steps haltingly, bumping into regular things, temporarily deceived and bewildered. In a theological sense, the poems lack grace and light. They do not seem to contemplate the doctrines of the Christian church, what might be call "revealed" truths, those that offer spiritual light. Thomas's poems in large part draw on human experience that may or may not precede the reception of divine grace; they explore darkness as a fact of the world and as a spiritual condition. The poem "Groping,"[22] from a 1978 collection, contains the lines,

> For some
> it is all darkness; for me, too,
> it is dark.

In nature, darkness is the order of each day, a welcome rest to those who have shelter against it, an uncomfortable difficulty to those who must stand alone in it. In theological language, darkness is a metaphor for the atmosphere in which sinful human beings live. One may be in a familiar place and still be quite lost, imprisoned, anxious, depressed, alone. In the dark, one's senses may be sharpened or one's senses may fail all together. Of course, in the dark, one may also find peace and rest not available in the light of day.

Darkness falls on all of us, again and again, yet each dark-fall contains its own redemption. Good things happen in sheltering darkness. Shade gives a thin shield of darkness to protect from blazing light. A seed and a fetus require a certain darkness for maturation and development. Likewise, the spirit needs periods of darkness for its own growth.

One kind of spiritual darkness that Thomas often seems to have in mind surrounds an inward journey, a Kierkeaardian examination of the sinful self. In a Christian paradox, on this dark journey one may receive grace. Divine grace has become incarnate in the world: the doctrine of the nativity affirms the planting on earth of the seed of God. The death, burial, and flowering of that seed offers a model of the godly life that dies to sin and rises renewed. So the darkness drives the faithful to their knees, not only in bewilderment and confession, but in prayer and thanksgiving as well.

In his poem "Kierkegaard" Thomas reflects upon the Danish philosopher's tragic turning from his beloved Regina, whose

> . . . hair was to be
> The moonlight, towards which he leaned
> From darkness.

This personal tragedy, combined with public ridicule and the Danish press's satire and scorn, drove Kierkegaard's thoughts deeply inward even as it buckled his knees. So that

> . . . wounded, he crawled
> To the monastery of his chaste thought
> To offer up his crumpled amen.[23]

An early verse drama, "The Minister,"[24] contains a concise and tragic anthropology:

> His slow wound deepens with the years,
> And knows no healing only the sharp
> Distemper of remembered youth.

A human life is full of calamity; then it ends. Contemplating this can be maddening and terrifying, or it can be sweet, with death a dessert sweeter still. In "The Priest," Thomas imagines a priest on his parish rounds, ministering to his flock in the gathering darkness. His course is similar to Kierkegaard's. Though the public and the press do not watch the village priest the way they watched Kierkegaard, the priest is nevertheless rejected and somewhat despised for the truth he bears through his office, even as his essential services are desired by those who despise him:

The priest picks his way
Through the parish. Eyes watch him
From windows, from the farms;
Hearts wanting him to come near.
The flesh rejects him.

Priests have a long way to go.
The people wait for them to come
To them over the broken glass
Of their vows, making them pay
With their sweat's coinage for their correction.

He goes up a green lane
Through growing birches; lambs cushion
His vision. He comes slowly down
In the dark, feeling the cross warp
In his hands; hanging on it his thought's icicles.

'Crippled soul', do you say? Looking at him
From the mind's height; 'limping through life
On his prayers. There are other people
In the world, sitting at table
Contented, though the broken body
And the shed blood are not on the menu'.[25]

He makes his pastoral calls in daylight, although as he "picks" his way through the village it seems somehow like night. On his way, he notices lambs, the gentlest symbols of sacrifice and of Christian salvation. He returns home at night, leaning on a cross. Supported by that limb of life, the priest, like Kierkegaard, appears to be crippled. Yet, though many have no need for his words and no conception of his Lord, he is able to kneel one step back from the pit of despair and, like Kierkegaard, to utter an affirmation:

'Let it be so', I say. 'Amen and amen'.

The Tree

Images of trees and of wooden crosses appear throughout Thomas's poems. An example of wood as the object of attention and devotion has already been noted in the poem "Kneeling." Wood also provides other central images for Thomas: the tree in its natural setting represents the origin of life, while the tree in the form of the empty cross provides a complex symbol of the absence of God, and of the paradoxical presence of God to the eyes of faith. For Thomas, the cross signifies both a remnant of natural power and a more strictly Christian sign of sacrificial death of the self.

Clearly, Thomas holds the formulaic belief that as humanity acquires more ability to affect the earth—through technological and mechanical prowess—the silence of God deepens. This belief includes the corollary that God's silence increases human loquaciousness, and vice versa. Julian Gitzen writes that Thomas

> has maintained consistency throughout his poetic career: he has remained from the first an enemy of "progress" insofar as progress is identified with increased mechanization, the relentless expansion of gadgets, the triumph of materialism and the crumbling of regional customs and values in the face of televised internationalism.[26]

For Thomas, the cross participates in ancient power because it is made of wood. Gerardus van der Leeuw traces an ancestry of belief in the power vested in a dead tree:

> It is remarkable . . . that in Egypt and Greece it was usually the barren, dead tree that was believed to be the bearer of potency of the god: the secret of the tree, which so deeply impressed man, was that of the vicissitudes of life and death.[27]

In Thomas's poetry, pagan beliefs—some of them probably rooted in his native Wales—marry Christian doctrine in a spiritual co-mixture. The two threads of belief share the cross/tree planted in the world as the point of meeting along their axis of meaning.

In the poem "Adder," Thomas writes of a small snake that

> It is scion
> of a mighty ancestor
> that spoke the language
> of trees to our first
> parents . . .[28]

The "language" of trees is equivalent to its cycle of life, from the soil to a seed, to leaves, buds and bark, and then to ash and decay. But Thomas means more than merely the language of biology. He means as well, if not primarily, the religious concept of sin that was "taught" by the serpent in Genesis 2–3 and has its roots in idolatry. The serpent began to teach our biblical ancestors to transgress the boundaries given by God, promising them a transcendent power able to tower above the earth and soar to the sky.

Apart from Thomas's imaginative association of the tree with the Christian doctrine of sin, the tree remains a symbol of the mysterious power of nature. A long, dense human story could be written from the impulse to revere the tree and objects made from it. To this day objects made of wood retain slivers of their ancient meaning. Van der Leeuw comments:

> . . . the evolution from Nordic tree worship through the Christian iconography of the Tree of Life and the wooden cross . . . goes directly to the heart of one of our most powerful yearnings: the craving to find in nature a consolation for our mortality.[29]

Throughout the seasons of the Christian year, the impulse to revere objects made of wood finds its expression not only in veneration of the cross, but also in remembering Noah's ark, the manger of Bethlehem, the altar of the Eucharist, and the coffins of saints, to name a few.

Thomas experiences the power of the tree as part of the mystery of God's word and of the mystery of nature. Often the two are inseparable. In an autobiographical essay in 1986 he wrote:

> The problem I have always had difficulty in coming to terms with is the majesty and mystery of the universe and

the natural world as a kind of symbol of God over against the domesticating urge in man. To kneel in my furnished room with its chairs and books, and then to look out and see Orion and Sirius rising above the bay makes it difficult to hold the two in proportion . . . it would seem that the deity has chosen to mediate himself to me via the world, or even the universe of nature. . . .[30]

The first section of Thomas's volume *Counterpoint*[31] is introduced by a poem entitled "BC," which recalls an early stage of evolution of the human species. In the second part of this poem he writes:

If you can imagine a brow puckered
Before thought, imagine this page
Immaculately conceived
In the first tree, with man rising
From on all fours endlessly to begin
Puckering it with his language.

Not only does Thomas envision the natural world as a tree-filled sanctuary, he also would populate his trees with pilgrim birds and a cacophony of bird song.

Broad sanctuaries and wide vistas fit his poetic, religious, and aesthetic sensibilities. Thomas knows that human beings create small and limited spaces for themselves: rooms, churches, religions, nations, systems of thought and morality. We are more or less at home in these spaces. Yet some people, including poets such as Thomas, understand that human constructions cannot contain everything we need or all that our hearts can comprehend. Even after we have built and praised our monuments and celebrated our achievements, something in us wonders with King Solomon,

Will God indeed dwell on the earth? Even heaven and the highest heaven cannot contain you, much less this house. . . .[32]

It could be said that Thomas repeats Solomon's question a number of times in his poems, aware as he is of living under limits and longing for some limitless heaven.

The tree, for Thomas, is not only a token of undifferentiated primeval power, it stands as well for a doctrine of Christology deriving from the action located on—and the absence made plain by—the cross. Often in Thomas's poems, the cross will have no figure upon it, remaining bare. One of several exceptions occurs in "Contacts":

> But for the one
> who is homeless
> there is only the tree with the body
> on it, eternally convulsed
> by the shock of its contact
> with the exposed nerve of love.[33]

Remembering Augustine's famous line about restless hearts resting "only in Thee," one could substitute *restless* for Thomas's *homeless*. Gazing on the cross/tree draws our restless eyes home. The cross becomes not only the primeval home of humankind, the source of our language, but also our devotional and ritual center. This tree is the home of God, where God is known as the Word, is born, and dies at the failure of our words.

> So God is born
> from our loss of nerve?
> He is the tree that looms up
> in our darkness, at whose feet
> we must fall to be set again
> on its branches on some April day
> of the heart.[34]

Thomas would have us look beyond the cross also, widening our focus to include the landscape surrounding it. The Welsh countryside, his own local landscape, appears in many of his poems. The stark and beautiful "Pietà" draws such a scene with unsentimental compassion:

> Always the same hills
> Crowd the horizon,
> Remote witnesses
> Of the still scene.

And in the foreground
The tall Cross,
Sombre, untenanted,
Aches for the Body
That is back in the cradle
Of a maid's arms.[35]

"Where is the body?" This is Mary Magdalene's question recorded in John 20. The presumed disappearance of Jesus' body adds anguish to the loss felt by his friends. When Mary recognizes Jesus in the garden, she reaches out for him. Jesus pulls back:

> Jesus said to her, "Do not hold on to me, because I have not yet ascended to the Father. But go to my brothers and say to them, 'I am ascending to my Father and your Father, to my God and your God.'"

Jesus instructs Mary to go and tell the other disciples of his presence. He will leave them again in a short time when he ascends to his Father. Though there is physical absence after his ascension, love's promise of presence is completed in the spiritual communion of the first Christians. Absence becomes a way to real presence. Simon Schama writes that

> . . . to a Lakota shaman . . . invisibility was a sign of presence, not absence. . . . The Great Spirit, Wakonda, was indistinguishably embedded with the rock and the scree. To feel its presence and that of all the ancestors buried in such a place required only a kind of respectful annihilation of the human self. . . .[36]

To Christians, the cross is the central spiritual "place," independent of time and geography, the emblem of sacrificial love. The event accomplished on the cross is a story that seems like a long-running rumor. Without verification of the events, without proof or substantiating signs of the cross's claims, the symbol stands as a mystery of life beneath the shroud of darkness and death that surrounds all life. Faith reaches out like an infant, without words, to pull the darkness in to itself, finding in this gesture enough comfort for the night.

1. R. S. Thomas, *Poems of R. S. Thomas* (Fayetteville: The University of Arkansas Press, 1985), 61.

2. This usual reading of Thomas's religious poems is summarized at length by W.J. Keith in the *Dictionary of Literary Biography, Vol. 27: Poets of Great Britain and Ireland, 1945–1960* (Villanova University: Gale Research, 1984), 346–356.

3. In *Miraculous Simplicity: Essays on R. S. Thomas*, ed. William V. Davis (Fayetteville: The University of Arkansas Press, 1993), 174.

4. Psalm 27:14.

5. Romans 8:22–23.

6. I am grateful to Professor Edward Hobbs, who preached at St. Mary's Episcopal Church, Newton Lower Falls, Massachusetts, on the meaning of Christian service and waiting in relation to Mary and Martha, as recorded in Luke 10.

7. Thomas, *Poems*, 134.

8. Davis, *Miraculous Simplicity*, 110.

9. Oliver Clément, *The Roots of Christian Mysticism* (New York: New City Press, 1993), 195.

10. Dom Gregory Dix, *The Shape of the Liturgy* (New York: The Seabury Press, 1983), 13.

11. Thomas, *Poems*, 148.

12. Thomas, *Poems*, 143.

13. Thomas, *Poems*, 21.

14. Evelyn Underhill, *Worship* (New York: Harper & Brothers, 1937), 205.

15. *Miraculous Simplicity*, 25.

16. Habakkuk 2:20.

17. 1 Kings 19.

18. Clément, 30.

19. Philip Larkin, *Collected Poems* (London: The Marvell Press, 1989), 97.

20. Thomas, *Poems*, 25.

21. Simone Weil, *Gravity and Grace* (London: Routledge, 1963), 104.

22. Thomas, *Poems*, 113.

23. Thomas, *Poems*, 48.

24. Thomas, *Poems*, 6ff.

25. Thomas, *Poems*, 60.

26. *Miraculous Simplicity*, 174.

27. Gerardus van der Leeuw, *Religion in Essence and Manifestation* (Princeton: Princeton University Press, 1986), 56.

28. Thomas, *Poems*, 170.

29. van der Leeuw, 14.

30. *Miraculous Simplicity*, 19.

31. R. S. Thomas, *Counterpoint* (Newcastle: Bloodaxe Books, 1990), 8.

32. 1 Kings 8:27.

33. Thomas, *Poems*, 180.

34. Thomas, *Poems*, 172.

35. Thomas, *Poems*, 48.

36. Simon Schama, *Landscape and Memory* (New York: Vintage Press, 1995), 398.

Chapter 7

Truly, truly, I say to you, unless a grain
of wheat falls into the earth and dies, it
remains alone; but if it dies, it bears
much fruit.

John 12:23

'Is my team ploughing,
    That I was used to drive
And hear the harness jingle
    When I was man alive?'

Ay, the horses trample,
    The harness jingles now;
No change though you lie under
    The land you used to plough.

A. E. Housman (1859–1936)
"Is My Team Ploughing?"

The oaks, how subtle and marine,
Bearded, and all the layered light
Above them swims; and thus the scene,
Recessed, awaits the positive night.

Robert Penn Warren (1905–1989)
"Bearded Oaks"

·7·

To Know the Dark: Wendell Berry

More than thirty years ago the French cultural historian Philippe Ariès wrote that

> death has become a taboo, an unnamable thing and, as formerly with sex, it must not be mentioned in public. Nor must other people be forced to mention it ... death has replaced sex as the principal prohibition.[1]

What Ariès observed remains generally true today within Western culture. Wide rivers of money flow constantly into medical research toward the goal of prolonging life. Death occurs as an instance of the failure of medical technology and science, and is therefore denied an honored place.

Christian writers provide a corrective to our death-denying culture. The Christian faith does not receive death as a shameful human failure or as a final fact shrouded in silence. Faith faces death. The Roman Catholic theologian Hans Küng, in his book *Eternal Life?*, endorses and repeats a statement by the Protestant theologian Heinz Zahrnt:

> When all the guarantees, supports and bridges break down by which we strive to secure our life, when we lose all the ground from under our feet and sink into complete unconsciousness, from which we can no longer relate to any of our fellow human beings and none of them can relate to us, then faith becomes total, then it is revealed as what it always is or should be by its very nature: reliance on God alone and consequently in life and death.[2]

The Protestant theologian Paul Tillich similarly emphasized the interconnection of life and death:

> death is not merely the scissors which cuts the thread of our life . . . it is rather one of those threads which are woven into the design of our existence, from its very beginning to its end.[3]

The poetry of Wendell Berry accomplishes a weaving of the threads of life and death to which Tillich refers. Berry's poetic voice springs up from the land of his Kentucky farm. While Geoffrey Hill's poems move down carefully through the layers of the history of language, Berry's poems sink into the soil of his farm and move with the measured pace of a man treading unpaved paths on his own land, being aware of nature, of light, and of the meaning of darkness.

Berry's commitment to the traditional belief that art and life should hold thought and action together gives his poems a consistent, rounded shape. This comprehensive way of looking at the world resounds through his work, as does reverence, which he has defined as "wholeness of understanding." By intentionally noting and participating in the patterns of life and death, he sees the glory in what others have done and left behind. Of special value to him are the promises kept through generations, promises that promote human virtues and provide the field for sacred vows and treasured memories. He bows to past knowledge and experience, even though such experience may not be his own. With the eyes of faith, he and his readers are then able to receive the grace of those experiences as a gift.

Living and Dying on the Land

The agricultural *milieu* in which the Gospels were written assumes a deep familiarity with planting and growing. Jesus taught in parables employing images of sowing seeds, of wheat fields, and of reaping, all of which would have been instantly understood by his hearers. In a technological society such deep recognition cannot be assumed.

There is a time in spring when the seed has been sown but has not yet sprouted. For a while the seed must lie in darkness below the ground. This seed—last year's grain—remains buried and dead until it sprouts, generating the hope of a new harvest. As a farmer, Berry understands darkness both as a time of rest and as a condition requiring faith in the next season of change and growth. He faces darkness and death with the even assessment of a farmer at home on the land, knowing that as night complements and completes day, so death completes and even nourishes life. Berry would agree with Sherwin Nuland, who writes in *How We Die:*

> . . . death is easiest for those who during their lives have given it most thought, as though always to be prepared for its imminence . . . experienced life more fully because of the constant awareness that it may soon come to an end.[4]

Berry experiences life as a farmer and as a writer within a complex web of agricultural and literary relationships. Human and non-human life entwine within the fabric of his imagination. Through his physical labor on the farm he draws his favored draft horses into partnership. In his imaginative writing he converses with literary ancestors. Furthermore, in his rooted life he joins in circles of life and death. Those who have died serve the living as they nourish the soil. The living serve the unborn by their stewardship of the land. The circle of love is completed when the living honor the dead through the same service.

In his writing Berry consistently defies fashions and trends. With steady intelligence and imagination he attends instead to the cycles and seasons of life. In an essay on contemporary poetry, he speaks with ideological firmness in our time of malleable cultural relativism:

> Contemporaneity, in the sense of being "up with the times," is of no value. Wakefulness to experience—as well as to instruction and example—is another matter. . . . The job now is to get back to that perennial and substantial world in which we really do live, in which the foundations of our life will be visible to us, and in which we can accept our responsibilities again with the conditions of necessity and mystery. In that world, all wakeful and responsible people, dead, living, and unborn, are contemporaries. And that is the only contemporaneity worth living.[5]

Berry believes in the power of poetry to deepen an appreciation of the rooted lifestyle he favors. Poetry acquires this power through the combustion generated when language and the imagination interact. He writes:

> To preserve our places and to be at home in them, it is
> necessary to fill them with imagination. To imagine as
> well as see what is in them . . . to see them first clearly
> with the eyes, and then to see them with the imagination
> in their sanctity, as belonging to the Creation . . .
> perhaps we may begin to see [life] in its sacredness, as
> unimaginable gift, as mystery—as it was, is, and ever
> shall be, world without end.[6]

A natural continuation of Berry's statement would be that the same imaginative poetry that helps us see the sacredness of life may also enable us to accept death as part of the same mysterious gift.

> We do not live to ourselves, and we do not die to our-
> selves. If we live, we live to the Lord, and if we die, we die
> to the Lord; so then, whether we live or whether we die,
> we are the Lord's.[7]

Home

A primary focus of Berry's thought and art is his understanding of *home*. He places high value on knowing where and to whom one belongs. For Berry, home means more than a certain piece of land, or the house built upon it. The word resonates through all the layers of culture and relationships that have been experienced there, over time. Residents include not only the living neighbors, but also the men and women of past generations who were at home in the same place and whose bodies now rest in the soil. The third article of the Apostles' Creed, "We believe in the communion of the saints," resonates with Berry's sense of the saints of earth, those whose presence remains all around his home.

The multiple overtones of *home* include peace, the deep, the womb, Eden, and heaven. It is sometimes said of a person who dies that he or she has gone home. In rural culture, before gatherings to honor the dead moved to public funeral homes, family and friends arrived at the home of the one who had died to sit with the bereaved for a while. The home served as a sanctuary to receive the dead and provided a locus for memory, as demonstrated by the closing lines of a poem by Seamus Heaney, describing a child's body brought home:

> Next morning I went up into the room. Snowdrops
> And candles soothed the bedside; I saw him
> For the first time in six weeks. Paler now,
>
> Wearing a poppy bruise on his left temple,
> He lay in the four-foot box as in his cot.
> No gaudy scars, the bumper had knocked him clear.
>
> A four-foot box, a foot for every year.[8]

For Berry, home refers to a primary and essential human attachment. He writes:

> I am endlessly in need of the work of poets who have
> been concerned with living in place, the life of a place,
> long-term attention and devotion to a settled home and
> its natural household, and hence to the relation between
> imagination and language and a place.[9]

Not all of us live Berry's re-rooted life. Most of us are transient. We change our addresses in pursuit of the needs of our jobs and families. The demands our children place upon us require that we keep up with consumer trends and hold suburban values. For those of us without a Kentucky farm to return to, *home* may stand for some other permanent feature of life.

Christian readers might appropriate Berry's understanding of home through the traditions of the church. The faith expressed in the creeds, for example, might become a kind of "place" in which to rest and grow throughout one's years. Berry's planted perspective may help the faithful reclaim an earthbound joy in the span of human life. Images of home and rootedness in "Stay Home,"[10] for instance, appear no less powerful from this perspective. In the first stanza, he imagines the fields and pasture land on his farm, concluding with the refrain:

I am at home. Don't come with me.
You stay home too.

The second stanza imagines a woodland scene and ends with
the same refrain:

I will be standing in the woods
where the old trees
move only with the wind
and then with gravity.
In the stillness of the trees
I am at home. Don't come with me.
You stay home too.

Without spiritual sentimentality or nostalgia, Berry reminds
his readers that they are children of earth as well as children of
the spirit, and that they share the earth with other creatures.

Living with Animals

Draft horses are the muscle partners of Berry's farm. He has
written many essays in promotion of farming methods that use
the power of horses. In "Horses,"[11] he writes:

When I was a boy here,
traveling the fields for pleasure,
the farms were worked with teams.
As late as then a teamster
was thought an accomplished man. . .

A young draft horse is trained by hitching it to an older horse
in the field. Without having to bear the load, the young horse
feels how the experienced animal works: responding to the
driver, now pulling, now easing up, working in tandem with the
other pulling horse. As a boy, Berry was given the reins before
he knew that driving a team was considered work. In this
play/learning, the boy began to pick up a kind of native poetry:

I learned the other tongue
by which men spoke to beasts
—all its terms and tones.

Men working with boys, gently teaching them the ways of farming, men working with horses, horses working beside other horses, until men and horses die and new children and horses are born, to be apprenticed to those who learned before them the rounds of life and death—these are the natural circles of life and stewardship.

When tractors came to the farm, the music of this dance was supplanted by the sound of the revolution of engines:

> The songs of the world died
> in our ears as we went within
> the uproar of the long syllable
> of the motors. Our intent entered
> the world as combustion.

One language was replaced by another. The language of death and decay, of life and generations, was lost when machine power replaced the partnership of human and horse power:

> . . .Veiled in that power
> our minds gave up the endless
> cycle of growth and decay
> and took the unreturning way,
> the breathless distance of iron.

When Berry returned to his family farm after years in the city, he began to work the fields with horses again. The old music of the world came back to him. The pulling of the horses orchestrated the ancient ensemble of life and death in the decay and nurture of the soil. He ends the poem:

> This work of love rhymes
> living and dead. A dance
> is what this plodding is.
> a song, whatever is said.

Berry allows no romantic illusions. Enjoying interconnectedness with farm animals means colluding in their death. The life of one creature is sustained by the death of another in the order of creation. The first line of "For the Hog Killing"[12] plunges his readers into this stark truth:

> Let them stand still for the bullet, and stare the shooter in
> the eye. . .

A few lines down we begin to see the communal and biolog-
ical consequences:

> let this day begin again the change of hogs into people,
>   not the other way around,
> for today we celebrate again our lives' wedding with
>   the world,
> for by our hunger, by this provisioning, we renew the bond.

The image of the changing of hogs into people may seem
harsh to those of us with urban and suburban sensibilities. At
stake, to Berry, is an ethic of the chain of life, a chain in which
humanity serves as both a link and a steward.

Sentimentalizing animals, such as Walt Whitman did in
"Song of Myself,"[13] violates the created order and results in
defective art, according to Berry. He sees the desire to senti-
mentalize animals as a misguided attempt to defy death through
progress:

> The notion of romantic poets that they would like to turn
> and live with or as animals is a fantasy that has its coun-
> terpart in the notion of scientific and technological
> romantics that they will eventually turn and live with or
> as gods. Both notions would have been understood by
> Spenser or Shakespeare or Milton or Pope as sinful—not
> because either turning is possible, but because neither is.
> The evil of such notions is that they mislead us danger-
> ously about our own nature; they are illusions that
> corrupt and debase our humanity.[14]

While farm animals find their proper partnership with
humanity through their work, wild animals, pursuing their
instincts, relate to human beings in another way. Wild animals
participate in an uncultivated world with its own features and
order that intersects the world in which we grow our food and
work our land. Berry celebrates the solace the wild things offer:

> When despair for the world grows in me
> and I wake in the night at the least sound
> in fear of what my life and my children's lives might be,
> I go and lie down where the wood drake
> rests in his beauty on the water, and the great heron feeds.
> I come into the peace of wild things. . . .[15]

The peace of wild things springs from the absence of striving to be other than who they are. The wood duck does not desire to become a great heron. The great heron does not desire to become a bald eagle. They are in *place*, and therefore at peace.

Power

Berry fully understands that contemporary humanity has no hope of living with the same contentment as that of wild things. Human ambition and pride, including his own, darken the planet. Berry's poetry shows its dark side and its prophetic voice most clearly in denouncing the ambition and striving that he finds endemic in cities. On the farm he has tuned his life to the close ecological harmonies of earth; in cities the music of the earth has been buried beneath towers of steel and other monuments to ambition and dominance. Berry's voice takes on a prophet's despair: how may people who seek power through politics or economics see themselves as creatures of earth? He writes in "The Want of Peace,"[16]

> All goes back to the earth,
> and so I do not desire
> pride of excess or power,
> but the contentments made
> by men who have had little. . . .

In his letter to the Philippians, the Apostle Paul wrote about peace that passes all understanding.[17] Such a peace passes Berry's understanding, though, as has been shown, it seems not to elude the wood duck and the heron:

> I lack the peace of simple things.
> I am never wholly in place.
> I find no peace or grace.

The final lines show the poet as unsympathetic to the economies of industry:

> We sell the world to buy fire,
> our way lighted by burning men,
> and that has bent my mind
> and made me think of darkness
> and wish for the dumb life of roots.

To Berry, "the dumb life of roots" stands for life in an earlier, agricultural, place-honoring time, when humanity was "rooted" to the land and knew a "root" way of living on this planet. Human beings who are planted and rooted on earth have a proper relationship with their environment in life and in death. The wish for a rooted life may also include a wish for a final peace in a known grave, where biological processes slowly take life apart in order to give back life. Reminding readers of this relationship is the work of a moralist.

Like Geoffrey Hill, Wendell Berry is a literary moralist. The two write from different points of view—one from the towers of academia, the other near the furrows of farm fields—but both poets see an organic connection between words and life. An incarnational principle, if not identical with, at least very much like, the one at the heart of the Christian faith, gets full development in both poets. However, the thought in Berry's poems stays centered in the body, in the ground, in the natural order of things, and never rises to pure or transforming spiritual thought. In his poetry, Berry knows nothing more than what the trees outside his window know.

Berry knows the darkness that nourishes, and, like Hill, has witnessed another kind of darkness that devours. In "Dark with Power,"[18] from a 1968 volume, Berry wrote a protest of the war in Vietnam, cast in terms of Berry's Jeffersonian ideal of the family farmer, in this case, referring to the farmers and villagers of Vietnam. The war becomes a demonic table, set outside the simple economies of these villages and farms. The table serves international appetites for power; destruction feeds there, devouring life without serving life. Berry then reminds us that destructive appetites seek gratification in the United States as well as in Vietnam:

Dark with power, we remain
the invaders of our land, leaving
deserts where forests were,
scars where there were hills.

Berry knows that the craving for domination, fed by death, is hardly limited to governments and military actions on a global scale. Local and personal lives demonstrate the same trait and the same desires:

Fed with dying, we gaze
on our might's monuments of fire.
The world dangles from us
while we gaze.

Our technological, military, economic, even personal might builds monuments of fire, creations that assure their own destruction. A self-sustaining cycle, this fire turns into itself. The conflagration of our own desires burns with the exercise of self-serving, dominating power.

There could hardly be a greater contrast than that between the fire generated by a profane craving for power and the purifying fire described by John the Baptist in Luke's Gospel, though both images disturb us. John prophesied that the Messiah would come as a farmer, with the word that burns with a *purifying fire* of the spirit:

His winnowing fork is in his hand, to clear his threshing
floor and to gather the wheat into his granary; but the
chaff he will burn with unquenchable fire.[19]

In response to John's prophecy, faith prays: *Thine* is the kingdom and the *power* and the glory.

Marriage

While the concept of home may be the most thoroughly explored within Berry's near-dozen books of poetry, the meaning of marriage follows closely upon it, both as an essential element in his reverent view of life and as a significant component of his understanding of death. Most especially in the collection

The Country of Marriage, but also in other volumes, Berry pon-
ders marriages. Beginning with his own marriage, he expands
the image to draw in a broader sense of marriage seen in the
communion between living things. In "The Law That Marries
All Things,"[20] he writes about what might be called a law of
combinates. Un-like things tend to combine:

> The cloud is free only
> to go with the wind.
>
> The rain is free
> only in falling.
>
> The water is free only
> in its gathering together,
>
> in its downward courses,
> in its rising into air.

Berry sees death as another combination of unlike things, or
another deep instance of marriage. In "A Marriage, an Elegy,"[21]
we read of a couple who are joined to the earth:

> They lived long, and were faithful
> to the good in each other.
> They suffered as their faith required.
> Now their union is consummate
> in earth, and the earth
> is their communion.

In the last section of "In Rain,"[22] circles of marriages are
interwoven in the fabric of life on earth:

> Marriages to marriages
> are joined, husband and wife
> are plighted to all
> husbands and wives,
> any life has all lives
> for its delight.
> Let the rain come,
> the sun, and then the dark,

for I will rest
in an easy bed tonight.

The night is comfortable to those who have made sacramen-
tal peace with the world.

The poem "Canticle,"[23] from an early collection of Berry's
poems, develops further the poet's local and incarnate percep-
tion of death as a stage in the natural order of things, not as an
event to be overcome. It begins:

What death means is not this—
the spirit, triumphant in the body's fall,
praising its absence, feeding on music.

As the bed receives the body for a night's rest and in the
morning returns a rested person, the familiar dark ground
accepts the dead, and mysteriously returns life.

Above these cycles of life and death stand a land's silent
sentries. A thorough theological anthropology of human life-
on-the-land informs Berry's work. Within his cosmography,
trees serve an important function as doors of access to the fun-
damental mystery of life.

Trees

Trees are Wendell Berry's icons. Imagine that these words,
written by Henri Nouwen about painted Russian icons, refer
rather to trees as Berry sees them:

At first they seem somewhat rigid, lifeless, schematic and
dull. They do not reveal themselves to us at first sight. It is
only gradually, after a patient . . . presence that they start
speaking to us.[24]

Mircea Eliade and others have written that in traditional
societies the tree symbolized the cosmic tree, the *axis mundi*.[25]
In some primitive rites shamans and mystics ascended to
heaven by climbing a sacred tree. Berry ascribes no ladder-like
meaning to trees, however. There is little ascending spiritualism
anywhere in his rooted and cultivated world view. Trees are not
immortal, but their long and impassive lives may inform and

expand a human perspective on life. They are an ancient arche-
type of our life, enlarged and heightened. In "Planting Trees,"[26]
Berry delights in acknowledging their longevity:

> I have made myself a dream to dream
> of its rising, that has gentled my nights.
> Let me desire and wish well the life
> these trees may live when I
> no longer rise in the mornings
> to be pleased by the green of them
> shining. . . .

Aging, the tree seems almost an elder partner of an aging
human being. In "The Old Elm Tree by the River,"[27] the poet
identifies with this deeply rooted neighbor. His own senses are
tuned to—almost in identity with—changes in the limbs and
the trunk of the old tree:

> Shrugging in the flight of its leaves,
> it is dying. Death is slowly
> standing up in its trunk and branches
> like a camouflaged hunter. In the night
> I am wakened by one of its branches
> crashing down, heavy as a wall, and then
> lie sleepless, the world changed.
> That is the life I know the country by.
> Mine is a life I know the country by.
> Willing to live and die, we stand here,
> timely and at home, neighborly as two men.

Yet the two "men" differ in one significant way: the human
man knows that he must die. Paul Tillich wrote:

> Man's knowledge that he has to die is also man's
> knowledge that he is above death. It is man's destiny
> to be mortal and immortal at the same time.[28]

The knowledge of death might darken human minds with
fear, or alternatively serve as a field for faith and a stage for the
imagination.

Darkness and Death

Death in the New Testament, especially in Paul's letters, may be all of these things: a judgment of sin, a separation from God, and the means of salvation. In the field of sacred history, Adam, who died, stands for the seed of death, while Christ, who rose from the grave, stands for the flower and fruit of life:

> . . . Christ has been raised from the dead, the first fruits of those who have died. For since death came through a human being, the resurrection of the dead has also come through a human being; for as all die in Adam, so all will be made alive in Christ.[29]

For Christians, death is the hub of the wheel of life: Christian teaching turns all around it. Berry entitled his 1982 collection of poetry *The Wheel*. The initial poem in that volume, "Requiem,"[30] ends with these lines:

> Now may the grace of death
> be upon him, his spirit blessed
> in deep song of the world
> and the stars turning, the seasons
> returning, and long rest.

Death is a real event, not an illusion of "passing away" or going on a long journey. Death means that a body has returned to the ground, or to the deep. In another chapel sermon, Tillich emphasized the utter seriousness of the creedal statement that

> Christ died and was buried: He was buried, He—His whole personality. . . . The same is true of us . . . we shall be buried. . . . Only if we take the *buried* in the gospel stories seriously can we evaluate the Easter stories. . . .[31]

Berry's "Canticle" and other poems take "the buried" seriously. They contemplate the darkness of real burial, in the ground, in terms of rural experience. In "Canticle" the sterile "black clothes of the priest" presiding at the funeral are set against the fertile blackness of the soil from which "Yellow flowers sprout . . . at the beginning of April." These flowers

. . . wait in their blackness to earn joy
by dying.

Darkness is the final and always present mystery of death.

Berry reminds his readers that we stand on this fertile mys-
tery-darkness, depend on it, are fed by it, and finally, return to
it. In "Enriching the Earth,"[32] the poet tells about sowing
clover and grass, winter grains, and various legumes, "their
growth to be plowed in to enrich the earth." What the farmer
plows back into the field serves the dark. Furthermore, the poet
himself is slowly returning to the soil, yet he does not find this
a dreadful thought:

. . . I am slowly falling
into the fund of things. And yet to serve the earth,
not knowing what I serve, gives a wideness
and a delight to the air. . . .

"To Know the Dark,"[33] from the same collection, seems like
a confession of faith in the goodness of darkness. The flesh and
the body, including the flesh and the body of earth, receive
affirmation in similar ways throughout Berry's poems:

To go in the dark with a light is to know the light.
To know the dark, go dark. Go without sight,
and find that the dark, too, blooms and sings,
and is traveled by dark feet and dark wings.

Berry's poetic voices oppose nearly all religious and cultural
symbols, except trees, that stand above the living earth, and its
creatures, as presumed markers of death and memorials to life.
Readers will hear a radical faith, active and alive at the grave
and in the ground, in these lines from "The Farmer among
Tombs:"[34]

I am oppressed by all the room taken up by the dead,
their headstones standing shoulder to shoulder,
the bones imprisoned under them.
Plow up the graveyards! Haul off the monuments!
Pry open the vaults and the coffins
so the dead may nourish their graves

and go free, their acres traversed all summer
by crop rows and cattle and foraging bees.

A similar poem, "The Farmer, Speaking of Monuments,"[35] reveals a piety of necessary stewardship, an ecology of humility in partnership with the land. Human beings cannot *leap* from their proper place on earth to another element—such as to a monument in the air—and expect to live *there* forever. Not even a writer's words on the page grant him immortality. Words crumble in their service of earthly and temporary purposes:

All his sentences serve an art of the commonplace,
to open the body of a woman or a field
to take him in. His words all turn
to leaves, answering the sun with mute
quick reflections.

All things tend to fall and return to the rich composite of earth.

Mortal and immortal, sinners and saints, holding the purifying fire of the word and participating in the self-consuming fire of destructive human tendencies, blessed by darkness and in fear of darkness, the sons and daughters of earth dance their days on the wheel of life. In his poem "The Wheel,"[36] couples join with other couples to form one community in the dance:

They move in the ancient circle
of the dance. The dance and the song
call each other into being. Soon
they are one—rapt in a single
rapture, so that even the night
has its clarity, and time
is the wheel that brings it round.
In this rapture the dead return.
Sorrow is gone from them.
They are light.

Berry has tuned his life to absorb this music. If we can quiet ourselves, and block out the squeal of technological advancement long enough to catch the countercultural music of his poems, we might enjoy a fine articulation of a way of life nearly gone from our country. One hopes that Berry's unwavering voice will be heard in this new century, if only as the lonely sound of one crying out from the Kentucky River Valley with a good word for rooted, responsible, ecological life, for the grace of death, and, indeed, for the grace of the life to come.

---

1. Philippe Ariès, "La mort inversee. Le changement des attitudes devant la mort dans les societes occidentales," *Archives Europeennes de Sociologie*, 8 (1967), 169–195.

2. Hans Küng, *Eternal Life?*, trans. by Edward Quinn (New York: Doubleday, 1984), 173.

3. Paul Tillich, *The Shaking of the Foundations* (New York: Alfred A. Knopf, 1948), 196.

4. Sherwin B. Nuland, M.D., *How We Die; Reflections on Life's Final Chapter* (New York: Alfred A. Knopf, 1994).

5. Wendell Berry, *Standing By Words* (San Francisco: North Point Press, 1983), 13.

6. Berry, *Standing by Words*, 90.

7. Romans 14:7–8.

8. Seamus Heaney, *Selected Poems 1966–1987* (New York: Farrar, Straus and Giroux, 1988), 9.

9. Berry, *Standing by Words*, 88.

10. Wendell Berry, *Collected Poems: 1957–1982* (San Francisco: North Point Press, 1985), 199.

11. Berry, *Poems*, 225–227.

12. Berry, *Poems*, 200.

13. Walt Whitman wrote in "Song of Myself":
> I think I could turn and live with animals, they are so placid and self-contained,
> I stand and look at them long and long.

14. Berry, *Standing by Words*, 168.

15. Berry, *Poems*, 69.

16. Berry, *Poems*, 68.

17. Philippians 4:7.

18. Berry, *Poems*, 67.

19. Luke 3:17.

20. Berry, *Poems*, 247–248.

21. Berry, *Poems*, 152.

22. Berry, *Poems*, 267–268.

23. Berry, *Poems*, 17.

24. Henri Nouwen, *Behold the Beauty of the Lord, Praying with Icons* (Notre Dame, Indiana: Ave Maria Press), 14.

25. Mircea Eliade, *The Myth of the Eternal Return* (Princeton: Princeton University Press, 1965), 12–13.

26. Berry, *Poems*, 155.

27. Berry, *Poems*, 145.

28. Tillich, 171.

29. 1 Corinthians 15:20–22.

30. Berry, *Poems*, 233.

31. Tillich, 166.

32. Berry, *Poems*, 110.

33. Berry, *Poems*, 107.

34. Berry, *Poems*, 105.

35. Berry, *Poems*, 139.

36. Berry, *Poems*, 261–262.

Afterword

Ancient Israel wondered and cried aloud in the words of one of her poets:

> Remember how short my time is—
> for what vanity you have
> created all mortals!
> Who can live and never see death?[1]

Hugh Kenner wrote, in a different mood but with a similar question, about one of the parables of Jesus:

> The words in the Parable are very simple: "a sower went out to sow his seed, and as he sowed some fell by the wayside, and it was trodden down. . . ." What does it mean? asks not What did you say? But To what end did you say it? . . . Part of the primitive fascination of a story is this, that we often cannot be sure why it has been told.[2]

We are not sure why the stories of life—created, repeated, remembered—have been told. The adventure of art sometimes finds inspiration in this territory of uncertainty. Religion stakes its claims there as well. In this inconstant universe, endings are as important as beginnings. The one turns into the other. The Jewish and Christian scriptures show that trust is important equipment for the journey through our uncertain days, and promises are the stars by which we navigate.

In a contribution to a recent volume of essays of philosophical and theological reflections on death, Harvard Professor Peter Gomes claims, contrary to the messages of our death-denying culture, that coming to terms with death is the business of religion, and, in particular, the central and proper work of the Christian church. A good life and a good death are inseparable goals; the certainty of death gives order to life. The Christian gospel cannot be heard in its fullness other than beside the grave. Gomes challenges us with these words:

> ... we will have to recover a language and reappropriate symbols with which to speak of death and dying within the context of living and meaning. ... This does not invite speculation about the life to come, despite the vivid examples of such speculation with which Christian theology is littered. We need only remember the Bible's reticence in that speculation. ...[3]

Some of our poets are out there writing in the dark, creating and recovering words and symbols of death in life. These literary artists know themselves as sons and daughters of the earth. Their poems are songs of the earth and not always the final word of gospel testimony. A poem by Denise Levertov offers a suitable encouraging last word:

> Keep writing in the dark:
> a record of the night, or
> words that pulled you from depths of unknowing,
> words that flew through your mind, strange birds
> crying their urgency with human voices,
>
> or opened
> as flowers of a tree that blooms
> only once in a lifetime:
>
> words that may have the power
> to make the sun rise again.[4]

---

1 Psalm 89:47–48.

2 Hugh Kenner, The Pound Era (Berkeley: University of California Press, 1971), 23.

3 Peter Gomes, "Death and the Believer: Death is Where We Start From" in If I Should Die, Leroy Rouner, ed. (Notre Dame: Notre Dame Press, 2001), 39–52.

4 Denise Levertov, Poems 1972–1982 (New York: New Directions Books, 1982), 261.

Suggested Readings

Wendell Berry
Collected Poems 1957–1982. San Francisco: North Point Press, 1985.
A Timbered Choir: The Sabbath Poems 1979–1997. Washington, DC: Counterpoint Press, 1998.

Scott Cairns
Philokalia. Lincoln, Nebraska: Zoo Press, 2002.
Recovered Body. New York: George Braziller, 1998.

Geoffrey Hill
The Triumph of Love. Boston: Houghton Mifflin, 1994.
Canaan. Boston: Houghton Mifflin, 1997.
New and Collected Poems 1952–1992. Boston: Houghton Mifflin, 1994.

Mark Jarman
Questions for Ecclesiastes. Ashland, Oregon: Story Line Press, 1997.
Iris. Ashland, Oregon: Story Line Press, 1992.
The Black Riviera. Middletown, Connecticut: Wesleyan University Press, 1990.

R(onald) S(tuart) Thomas
Poems. Fayetteville: University of Arkansas Press, 1985.

John Updike
Americana and Other Poems. New York: Knopf, 2001.